STRANGE VIEW
FROM A SKEWED ORBIT

Borgo Press Books by Ardath Mayhar

The Absolutely Perfect Horse: A Novel of East Texas (with Marylois Dunn)
The Body in the Swamp: A Washington Shipp Mystery [Wash Shipp #2]
Carrots and Miggle: A Novel of East Texas
The Clarrington Heritage: A Gothic Tale of Terror
Closely Knit in Scarlatt: A Novel of Suspense
Crazy Quilt: The Best Short Stories of Ardath Mayhar
Deadly Memoir: A Novel of Suspense
Death in the Square: A Washington Shipp Mystery [Wash Shipp #1]
The Door in the Hill: A Tale of the Turnipins
The Dropouts: A Tale of Growing Up in East Texas
The Exiles of Damaria: A Novel of Fantasy
Feud at Sweetwater Creek: A Novel of the Old West
The Fugitives: A Tale of Prehistoric Times
The Heirs of Three Oaks: A Novel of the Old West
High Mountain Winter: A Novel of the Old West
How the Gods Wove in Kyrannon: Tales of the Triple Moons
Hunters of the Plains: A Novel of Prehistoric America
Island in the Lake: A Novel of Native America
Khi to Freedom: A Science Fiction Novel
The Lintons of Skillet Bend: A Novel of East Texas
Lone Runner: A Novel of the Old West
Lords of the Triple Moons: A Science Fantasy Novel: Tales of the Triple Moons
Makra Choria: A Novel of High Fantasy
Medicine Dream: Being the Further Adventures of Burr Henderson
Messengers in White: A Science Fantasy Novel
Monkey Station: A Novel of the Future (Macaque Cycle #1; with Ron Fortier)
People of the Mesa: A Novel of Native America
A Planet Called Heaven: A Science Fiction Novel
Prescription for Danger: A Novel of the Old West
Reflections; & Journey to an Ending: Collected Poems
A Road of Stars: A Fantasy of Life, Death, Love, and Art
Runes of the Lyre: A Science Fantasy Novel
The Saga of Grittel Sundotha: A Science Fantasy Novel
The Seekers of Shar-Nuhn: Tales of the Triple Moons
Shock Treatment: An Account of Granary's War: A Science Fiction Novel
Slewfoot Sally and the Flying Mule: Tall Tales from Cotton County, Texas
Soul-Singer of Tyrnos: A Fantasy Novel
Strange Doin's in the Pine Hills: Stories of Fantasy and Mystery in East Texas
Strange View from a Skewed Orbit: An Oddball Memoir
Through a Stone Wall: Lessons from Thirty Years of Writing
Timber Pirates: A Novel of East Texas (with Marylois Dunn)
Towers of the Earth: A Novel of Native America
Trail of the Seahawks: A Novel of the Future (Macaque Cycle #2; with R. Fortier)
The Tulpa: A Novel of Fantasy
Two-Moons and the Black Tower: A Novel of Fantasy
Vendetta: A Novel of the Old West
Warlock's Gift: Tales of the Triple Moons
The World Ends in Hickory Hollow: A Novel of the Future
A World of Weirdities: Tales to Shiver By

STRANGE VIEW FROM A SKEWED ORBIT

AN ODDBALL MEMOIR

by

Ardath Mayhar

THE BORGO PRESS

An Imprint of Wildside Press LLC

MMIX

Copyright © 1996, 2009 by Ardath Mayhar

All rights reserved.
No part of this book may be reproduced in any form
without the expressed written consent
of the author and publisher.
Printed in the United States of America

www.wildsidepress.com

FIRST EDITION

CONTENTS

Introduction 7

Chapter One: In the Beginning Was Family 9
Chapter Two: The Conformity Machine, 1936-1947 22
Chapter Three: My Very Strange Name—and Nature ... 31
Chapter Four: Serpents 37
Chapter Five: The Cabin 43
Chapter Six: The Farm/Dairy, 1942-1957 53
Chapter Seven: Taking Off 55
Chapter Eight: Wolves and a Tornado 58
Chapter Nine: Context Shapes the Writer 61
Chapter Ten: Backing into Marriage, 1957 63
Chapter Eleven: Joe 66
Chapter Twelve: Our Own Oregon Trail, 1968 68
Chapter Thirteen: Don't Threaten a Texas, 1970 77
Chapter Fourteen: Going Home Again, 1975 81
Chapter Fifteen: A Fowl Story 83
Chapter Sixteen: Bookstore and Rebellion 86
Chapter Seventeen: Interviews 90
Chapter Eighteen: Letters 98
Chapter Nineteen: Personal Philosophy 150
Chapter Twenty: Who Creates Victims? 151

Chapter Twenty-One: Most Recent Years 157
Chapter Twenty-Two: A Final Note as of 2008 159

A Bibliography of the Books of Ardath Mayhar,
    Compiled by Robert Reginald 160
About the Author 167

INTRODUCTION

For decades I resisted the idea of writing an autobiography, although my friend Evelyn, with whom I shared many years in a newspaper proof room, urged me to write one. I insisted, and this was very true, that the main reason for writing at all is to find out what happened to interesting people who wander up the back roads of your mind. Yet I kept thinking of incidents I have experienced that were funny or strange or otherwise interesting, and I would put them into my computer as they occurred to me.

I still am not interested in writing an official autobiography, created according to rules (that is one of my strongest traits, anyway). However, I find that I have accumulated quite a lot of material in bits and pieces, and I have put these scraps together as nearly chronologically as can be done with matters that each may cover years and years. As I did this, I found other things occurring to me, and I wrote them also as individual essays or as connective tissue.

So here is a sort of mosaic of a strange family and life of an even stranger old lady. If it makes any sense at all, that can only be accidental, for much of it has been the result of sheer gutting it out in difficult circumstances.

Enjoy!

—Ardath Mayhar
Chireno, Texas
April, 2009

CHAPTER ONE

IN THE BEGINNING WAS FAMILY

JOSEPH GUY ELLINGTON

My grandfather was born and reared in Shelbyville, Texas, where the school was an unusually good one. A couple from New England had come to Texas because of the wife's health problems, and their education was more extensive than was usual here in the middle of the nineteenth century. I think their name was DuPré or something similar. Their library was so extensive that they built a small house near their front gate and used it as a lending library for people in Shelbyville.

When Daddy Joe finished school, which consisted of only about eight grades, Mr. DuPré told his father that such a bright boy should not be wasted on farming or logging. He advised Grandpa Ellington to send him to the telegraphers' school in Atlanta, Georgia. Grandpa agreed, and when Joe finished his training, he went to work almost immediately for the Santa Fe Railroad as station agent in Timpson, Texas.

This would have been some time after 1890, for he married his cousin Julia Cannon in 1899, and they moved into the house he built only a block or two from the depot in Timpson. He worked as the station agent and telegrapher there for a number of years.

One night a coffin came in on a train and had to wait at the station to be picked up by another train. Daddy Joe was a funny little fellow (5'4" and wore a size 5 shoe), superstitious about dead people. He walked up to his house and got my mother, who was five years old at the time, to sleep on a bench in the depot and keep him company for the rest of the night. This would be in 1905, for my mother was born in 1900.

I don't know exactly when he left the Santa Fe to work for Gulf Oil at the Timpson pumping station, but it occurs to me that the oil fields were being developed in north Texas in the late Twenties and early Thirties. Possibly Gulf was in the process of laying pipeline, establishing pump stations, and staffing them and probably needed telegraphers badly. They may have offered him a better salary or simply intrigued him with a new challenge.

When I was a child in the early Thirties, he sometimes took me to work with him at the pump station, where I watched with interest as he oiled the smaller engines on the ground floor, which ran the huge pumps below, then went to check on the pumps set in cement some fifteen feet below ground level. The noise of those was enough to shake your bones and make your head reel. We would climb also onto the great round storage tanks, open a small hatch, and he would drop down a rod to measure the amount of oil inside.

Daddy Joe would go about his business with one ear cocked to the telegraph. I have seen him chuckle at some funny remark someone was sending over the wire, reading the code as easily as if it were spoken. The tank field was surrounded by a very deep ditch (probably fifteen or twenty feet deep) to catch oil in case of a leak. A metal bridge spanned this to connect the houses for the employees to the tank field. Though my grandparents were supposed to live in one of those houses, they "just happened" to spend most nights in the home in Timpson, a few miles distant.

There could have been no better granddad—he was really no older than I, and he could DRIVE!

JULIA GERTRUDE CANNON ELLINGTON

My grandmother was the thirteenth child of her parents. Her father, Ravenna Francis, was a Civil War veteran who returned with serious malaria, which often laid him low for months at a time. His wife and seven daughters (there were two sons, but one died very young and the other when he was grown, but still young) worked the farm they operated on shares. Julia finished the Shelbyville School, passed the teacher examination, and by the time she was seventeen she was teaching school.

She and my grandfather were cousins. He "picked her out" when they were children, and they married in 1899 when she was nineteen. In 1900 my mother was born, after a three-day labor that required three doctors to deliver the baby alive. Five years later she gave birth to another daughter, my Aunt Frances Virginia Ellington (Rose).

Julia was tall (about 5'9"), auburn-haired, gray-eyed. She loved music and wanted badly to learn to play the piano, but my mother was so upset when she practiced that she finally gave it up. That is probably why both her daughters were given musical educations at the Cincinnati College of Music. She used her creative energy to raise big gardens, crochet and embroider lovely handwork, raise gorgeous flowers. In the early days she also made all the family's clothing, milked a cow, churned and sold butter, and participated in church work.

She also had mood swings that, in the light of present knowledge, were probably periodic depression. Her background in the very primitive Methodism of the era may have contributed to that, for she was taught that many perfectly harmless things were major sins, and she was so intelligent that it probably created very real cognitive dissonance within her personality. (Incident: My mother found a playing card on the street, when she was small. My grandmother snatched it from her hand, threw it away, and in a distressed voice told her, "That thing is a SIN!")

She had chronic pain in her spleen. In the early Thirties X-ray became the medical fad of choice. Dr. Johnson got an X-ray machine and gave treatments for every sort of complaint. He boasted that Julia could stand a treatment for thirty minutes at a time. It is not surprising that in 1939 she became seemingly anemic and was eventually diagnosed with leukemia. After months of increasing weakness, she died in September of 1939.

She was a beautiful, intelligent, loving woman who was, I realize now, in some ways a victim of her generation and area.[1]

Ardath Ellington Hurst

My mother lived to be seventy-four and one-half years old. I thought for years that this would be the limit of my own lifespan, but it turns out to be an error.

She was a very creative person, more in crafts and creative housekeeping than otherwise, and she was not a writer, though her letters were terrific. She was educated to be a piano teacher and attended Cincinnati College of Music, where she got her certification before returning to Texas to teach piano in Nacogdoches, where her uncle was superintendent of schools.

She roomed in one of the big old houses that offered accommodations to teachers, and while there she made some life-long friendships among the teachers. The closest of these was with Margaret Lanier, who was like a member of our family, a sort of extra aunt.

That does not give nearly the scope of my mother's personality, however. She was the older of two daughters, and she and her father cooperated like father and son. She helped him with his farm, which was a sideline.

She did not marry until she was twenty-four years old. My father taught her to work with electrical systems. After that she wired my grandfather's house for electricity. She was a good mechanic, and one of my earliest memories is

---

[1] Much of my children's book, *The Lintons of Skillet Bend*, is based on my grandmother and her family.

of her sitting on the living room floor, with her vacuum cleaner reduced to its constituent parts, finding and repairing the problem and then putting it back together, after which it worked.

A colleague of my father (he was a traveling salesman) met him in a hotel down the country one day and told him he had seen my mother on the road to Timpson, down in the Naconiche Creek bottoms where she had car trouble. When he stopped to ask if he could help, she stuck her head out from under the car and said, "Thank you, but I just about have it fixed." And she did.

She loved the farm, once we moved there in 1942, and I can still see her running after a runaway calf, her skirt-tail snapping in the breeze. We all worked together in the fields and had great fun doing it. She was afraid of nothing, which is probably why none of her children were ever fearful.

She never wondered what people thought about what she did. When acquaintances told her she would be ostracized if she dated "that traveling salesman," she married him. She lived her life on her own terms as nearly as a person can, for she was completely honest and straightforward and never, as far as I know, damaged a living soul. That isn't to say she wouldn't have killed someone threatening her family, without a second thought, if that had been necessary. In many ways, I am grateful to note, I am very like her.[2]

---

[2] My horror novel, *The Wall*, contains much of my mother's character and personality in its protagonist—and her Grand-Aunt Annabelle.

BERT A. HURST

My father was intelligent, imaginative, and a lot of fun, the most inventive person I ever knew. He could set his mind on a project, design not only the project but the tools to build it with, and even make the tools to make the tools. Although he was, for the first twelve years of my life, a traveling salesman, the weekends were wonderful.

We spent most of those weekends at the cabin on my grandfather's farm, until I was about nine years old. Then my grandmother died, a victim of medical faddism. My grandfather followed her in 1941.

The beginning of the Second World War and gasoline rationing put an end to going back and forth the forty-some miles to the Cabin. We needed something closer to home to keep us busy and happy.

When he was a boy back in West Point, Mississippi, at the turn of the century, Dad's neighborhood was like a very large family. The back yards on one side of the street joined together, separated by low fences, and there my very young father and his dedicated contemporaries created a mini-amusement park, complete with roller-coaster, starting in one lady's upstairs porch, down to the lawn, up and over a fence, down again, over another fence, to end in a patch of bushes.

To this he added a "spinning jenny," which was a plank fastened at the middle to a stump or low post. Someone sat on either end, pushed with feet, and spun round and round. He also built a Ferris Wheel. I mean it: a real, two-seater, self-propelled, swivel-seated Ferris Wheel.

He decided to build us one in our back yard (we still lived in Nacogdoches, at that time), to make up for the loss of the cabin. The day the truck came with a pair of eight-by-eight-inch posts ten feet long, together with two-by-twelve planks twenty feet long, as well as some shorter boards, my brother and I were agog. There was a bag of hardware that jingled too. The wait until Saturday afternoon when Dad got home from his week on the road was interminable.

That was a magical weekend. Two teenaged neighbor boys added their young muscles and considerable agility to putting the thing together, boring holes in the centers of the twenty-foot boards, setting big steel washers on either side, then stringing them onto a steel rod that tied together the tops of the posts. Those were deeply sunk and well tamped, and the rod connected them some twelve or fourteen inches from the tops.

The seats were built with bars that locked across the front so nobody would fall out. My brother being three years younger and correspondingly smaller than I, his seat had a false bottom that could be loaded with bricks to equalize the weight. Once my brother got into his seat I pulled the other one down, got in, and kicked off. As we went over the top we "pumped," as you do in a swing, keeping it going as long as we had the energy.

My brother, of course, would curl up and ride at my expense, and there was no way on earth to get at him. If I had ever thought to take something up to drop on him when he was directly below it might have worked, but unfortunately I always remembered too late. Or perhaps fortunately. The damage that might be done to a child's head by a pebble dropped from twenty feet above might have been considerable.

Our teen-aged helpers were, of course, welcome to ride at any time, but it seems, looking back, that it was the construction rather than the use of the thing that fascinated them.

On the other hand, one morning a car pulled up in the drive and a woman and small girl got out. "My daughter is going crazy," she said to our mother. "We live on North Street (some three blocks distant) and she keeps seeing your children's heads coming up over the trees and going back down again. Curiosity is about to kill her."

Of course the child got a ride and went home thrilled to her bones.

It was the Ferris wheel, probably, that sparked the idea for a carnival/circus. The two of us were rather young to initiate that, but Larry and Billy, our neighbors, were quite capable of doing it. Our big yard, complete with a chinaberry tree that seemed designed for acrobatic monkey-shines, was just the right setting.

Buzz and I added what we could where we could (being born hams helped), and our mother contributed cookies and Kool-Aid®. And, of course, she supervised closely the Ferris wheel rides that ended the festivities. (That was in the days before people were terrified of being sued if a visitor stubbed a toe.)

For an admission of one penny each, I think our customers got their money's worth. We had no complaints that I recall, anyway, although one small neighbor boy went back to the Kool Aid® pitcher so many times that he had to be told firmly to stop.

That was a summer to remember as long as I live. The cool green lawn, the playhouse behind the garage where we had books, an old wind-up record player, and a couch to lie on while we read, live in my mind yet. The dog yard, where the English setters were kept, was beside the playhouse, a quarter-acre tightly fenced to keep the two setters we owned at that time inside.

We played baseball in the back yard, and when somebody hit a ball over the hedge into the vacant lot beside our acre of ground we'd let Whiz, the older dog, out to retrieve it. He always watched ball games with great attention, his ears cocked, his tail wagging mightily. He knew for a certainty that before we were done he'd probably have a good sniff through the tall weeds after our baseball. And he almost always did.

Whiz was my first brother. He was born when I was two, and one of my very early memories is of going out and sitting in the door of the doghouse (all of fourteen inches square) while the black, blind puppy wriggled his way over his seven siblings to find my lap.

We were best friends and companions as long as he lived, and when he died I spent much youthful anger and energy ill-wishing the man who killed him. That man died of pneumonia while in the Army in England, a few years later, and I have often wondered if my childish fury was powerful enough to give him a nudge in that direction.

The Fall when I was about to be three years old, my Dad often took the litter of pups, now getting near their full growth, and their mother, Mitzi, out into the woods on training runs. I had been reared with bird dogs. I knew how to point and how to back the dog who found the birds as well as Mitzi did.

One day Dad and Mem were coming along behind us as we (pups and I, followed by Mitzi) trotted up a crooked woods trail. We came around a bend to face a brush pile, and I went down in a point. Mitzi backed me, and Dad walked forward to kick up a covey of quail. I have often wondered if I missed my calling. I'd have made a wonderful bird dog.

It was Whiz who helped to rout the timber thief on Daddy Joe's farm, and it was he who accompanied most of the rambles my brother and I took through our grandfather's woods. It was an era when there was no thought of danger to children. We roamed the woods, the pastures, the creeks, and the thickets, finding wild flowers, hickory nuts, acorns, false indigo seed-pods. We would return to the cabin laden with oddments of treasure from the woods.

So well were we taught wood-craft that neither of us ever got a snakebite or even poison ivy. But a part of the confidence with which our parents let us wander freely out of their sight or even earshot must have been their great confidence in the solid common sense of old Whiz, who made a guardian not to be equaled.

Whiz's mother, Mitzi, was a sweet little bitch, the daughter of the great Nujim (a renowned English setter of field trial fame). Nujim's Texas Miss was her formal name, and she was older than I, being the first Christmas present my mother bought for my Dad the Christmas they had been married a year. She arrived in November by train from Virginia, having been unfed and neglected all the way and left in the cold rain.

Suffering from distemper, the pup was a nasty, shivering (expensive) mess when my mother picked her up at the depot. Mem had to put her in the house to save her, though neither of my parents approved of house dogs. Tempting her appetite with mixtures of egg, milk, and ground meat wasn't easy. Then it got easier. Then it became entirely too easy.

When Mitzi was quite well again, she still expected such meals, served in the house by an anxious "servant." My mother learned to deal with children while teaching the recalcitrant pup that she ate what she was given, or it was taken away and didn't come back until mealtime rolled around again. Elements of that process still were resonating through time when I reared children of my own.

The bird dogs' fall training and conditioning and then the fall quail hunts were a part of my childhood. The distinctive smell of a hunting vest with shotgun shells in the individual pockets on the front and shot quail in the pouch at the back is still plain in my nostrils. I have used bits and pieces of those early experiences in all sorts of ways, particularly when I deal with forests and meadows and making one's way through them in winter.

To this day, when I am too achy and my knees aren't up to long rambles any more, I have to have forest nearby. I am a woods-person, and there must be a wild spot within reach of my wheel chair (if and when).

But the bird dogs are long gone to their well deserved rewards, and the Ferris wheel was dismantled when we moved to the farm and ended its life usefully but unglamorously as part of the timbers of the big hay barn. *Sic transit Gloria mundi!*

But if I set my mind to it, I can still feel the triumphant out-swing at the top of the giant circle, the rush of air against my face as I begin the downward arc. I can smell freshly mowed Bermuda grass and the giddily mingled scents of four-o-clocks and angel trumpets on warm East Texas air.

For a short moment, I can be ten years old again, on top of the world, my parents still in place holding things together. I wouldn't go back in reality, but a short visit to that past always helps me gird up my loins and dive back into the battle of living.

Dad had a coronary infarction in 1949, and a neighbor who both dairied and was a medical technician helped take him to the hospital. She was sitting there beside his bed, anxious as all get-out, when he said, "Mrs. Nance, something doesn't smell right in this hospital."

She leaned forward, all attention. "What's that, Bert?"

"I can't smell any cow manure at all," he replied.

She lifted her foot. "I noticed I had some on my shoe as we came up the steps. You take a good sniff," she told him.

My mother's first letter after Dad went into the hospital for the last time (1971) is typical Dad. He had to have five pints of blood before they could go in to see what his problem was. The next morning a young man came in with a tray of vials to take blood.

Dad said, "You can have all you want, but it isn't really mine, just some other guy's I've been using." He was always cheerful and funny, right up to the end.

He left me the most valuable heritage possible—the ability to look at a problem, think it over, and SOLVE IT.[3]

---

[3] Uncle Sol, the storyteller in *Slewfoot Sally and the Flying Mule*, is my Dad, who was one of the great storytellers of all time.

CHAPTER TWO

THE CONFORMITY MACHINE

1936-1947

Being the descendant of mavericks has made life very interesting and independent. I cannot remember ever hearing anyone in my family ask the question, "What will people think?"

We didn't give a damn. Still don't. Never, I devoutly hope, will.

There must be some Crusader blood someplace back there, because both my grandmother and I possessed that trait to sometimes dangerous degrees. She was confined to some extent by her generation and her cultural background, which was fundamentalist Methodist backwoods East Texas, leavened by enormous amounts of common sense and creative intelligence.

I had no such inhibiting factors in my life. My rule, following that of my parents, has been, "If it's self respecting and doesn't hurt anybody, full speed ahead."

The Conformity Machine, otherwise known as the Public School System, did its best with me, but it had very resistant material to work with. Instead of emerging a well-rounded character, with all the sharp edges abraded away, I came out of the experience with all my awkward angles not only intact but more acute than ever.

The first grade was an eye-opener. After I'd been roaming the limitless fields of my own imagination, not to mention the woods of the grandparental farm, for six years, when I was almost seven my family moved to Center, Texas, where I began my school career.

It was 1936 by then, and the Depression was beginning to ease just a bit, but there were accounts in Center that were behind with the Levi Garrett Snuff Company, and the company wanted Dad on the spot to collect any money the businesses laid hand to.

We moved into a small frame house with an enormous back yard that sported a shed that Dad converted into a playhouse, a spacious dog yard, and a huge, double-trunked pine tree. Onto the lowest branches of the pine Dad attached one of his wonderful hand-made swings, this one a double one with facing seats, designed for both "swingers" to pump. My brother and I spent many a summer morning on the swing, and the year dad's brother, sisters, niece, and nephew visited us, the teenagers spent quite a bit of time there too.

We lived there for a year, during which period my mother was continually ill. The water, we finally decided, was the reason, and my granddad brought jugs of water to her regularly from his home in Timpson. As my brother was still quite small, I became skilled at helping with housework, learned to cook (to some extent), and felt very useful.

We lived about three blocks from the school, where I was enrolled in the first grade. I liked school fairly well, though it was certainly not as fascinating as the things going on in my mind.

The winter came. When my mother put long lisle stockings onto a squirmy little girl and set her off to walk to school, she should have expected me to arrive all but strangled, as those hose twisted around and around my legs.

I didn't do it on purpose. Those devilish contrivances almost seemed to be trying for my neck, though they never managed to twine that high before she gave up in disgust and put me in socks instead. I will remember lisle stockings as long as I live, for they were a torture that might have been recommended to the Inquisition without much alteration.

I passed directly under the windows of the jail on my way to school every day. My grandfather had a cousin who was there every Saturday night for being drunk in public, getting out each Monday. I kept wondering if he might stick his head up to the bars and yell at me. He never did, which was both a disappointment and a relief. It never occurred to me (and I think it never occurred to my mother) to be ashamed of him. I thought it was interesting to have kinfolk in jail.

Miss Martha (I don't recall her last name) was a very patient teacher, which was good, as I much preferred watching the matters playing themselves out in my mind to learning to write my name. It took a while before I mastered that art, and it never did come to seem terribly important.

Though my mother read to me and my brother regularly, and we hung on her words, I did not, oddly enough, learn to read before starting school. I was too busy seeing the pictures her words evoked inside my head to pay attention to the squiggles on the page. Reading, however, came easily, once I was given the phonic keys, and I took off well.

Of course, about the middle of the school year we moved back to Nacogdoches, where we preferred to live. I guess Dad got all the Company's money, though I never did ask him. Money wasn't then (and still isn't, sad to say) a motivating factor in my life.

Miss Bertha T. was my new teacher, and I went into a class of thirty or so strangers. Not that I minded—I don't remember a single child from school in Center, and only those in my first grade class in Nacogdoches who went through all the grades with me became real people.

Why? I think I'm not fully human. I observe from outside, mull over my observations, and turn them into tales. Because I had a highly retentive memory, learning was not difficult, and I did that without distracting my attention from my inner life. That was the important one.

At that point I was not aware that everyone didn't exist in that manner. Now I feel somewhat sad when I think of the feelings I must have injured along the way, through sheer absent-mindedness.

The rules of school always amused me highly. I wasn't a trouble-maker (imaginative children learn better ways to use their energies and their occasional hostilities), but I was certainly not a cooperator, either. What everyone was supposed to do together, in a "group manner," repelled me violently, in every way.

I hated "play period." I didn't like games. I ran for my own amusement, as much as my early-appearing trick knee allowed, and I did not scream. During play period I was very much in the position of a sixty-year-old lady forced to submit herself to the noise and chaos of a bunch of small children with whom she has neither sympathy nor anything at all in common.

Thirty years later, when my youngest son came home from his first day at school, raised his big brown eyes, and said in shocked tones, "Mama, some of those children cried!" I knew just how he felt. It made one ashamed to be numbered among the young of the species.

If I was never young, I never learned to grow old, either. Nothing the teachers or peers or anyone else said or did changed that, though I absorbed knowledge like a small, square sponge.

I suspect, at this point in my life, that some of my teachers may have become concerned to find such a child among their students. A loner from the word go, I did not participate voluntarily in group activities, or even to much extent under coercion. I didn't like competitions or sports or anything popular. If everyone else rafted merrily downstream, I swam doggedly upstream.

Only the fact that my mother, a former music teacher, knew and was friends with many of my teachers along the way saved me from possible disaster. If someone had tried to civilize me, it would have brought out my Berserker blood, I have no doubt.

Miss Margaret, long-time teacher and my mother's best friend, was a great help. Evidently she understood that this was one weird kid, and she made quiet suggestions instead of issuing stern orders when she visited us, which was often. She eased me into school life, for which I will always be grateful. I wonder now if she ran interference for me among other teachers who didn't know my family. I had very little static from any of my teachers along the way.

My elementary school teachers were brilliant women to whom no other career was open. None were married, for at that time it was against school policy in Nacogdoches for a married woman to teach here. All knew their subjects and provided their students with solid academic backgrounds, firm discipline, and excellent standards for both learning and self-control. Of my graduating class (1947) something like a quarter became teachers, which is a pretty good record.

We learned to be quiet when it was necessary, to concentrate upon material we must learn, and to memorize. Lacking the ability to memorize, no matter what liberal academics may claim, has to be a terrible disability. We did not suffer from that, and the capacity has been of utmost value throughout my life. Besides, anyone who doesn't learn the multiplication table by rote is going to regret it forever. A solid store of memorized poetry can serve you well, too, on sleepless nights, on long drives, or, as Vietnam captives learned, when enduring long captivity.

High School was a different matter. Though my teachers continued to be sympathetic to this duck in the chicken pen, there began to be peer pressure, though at that time (and perhaps still), I thought it unwarranted interference on the parts of really dumb people who hadn't a clue as to who and what I might be.

I should wear makeup? Why? To attract those pimply boys, whose main virtue seemed to be an ability to get around the good sides of math teachers?

I should cut off my long braids and curl my hair? What on earth for? I never applied for beautiful, which is a very good thing as it turned out. There was no time for such nonsense. I was busy with school, and after we moved to the farm I was busy milking cows by hand and baling hay and planting crops and generally helping to make our living.

When "normal" girls said, "When-I-grow-up-'n'-get-married" (all one word), I wondered what on earth they meant. I had no intention of marrying, ever, and anything leading to that state was a matter of total indifference to me then (and even now—my husband and I backed into each other, in a way, neither of us being interested in matrimony at the time, though we soon changed our minds).

As usual, I didn't give a bow-legged damn what other people were doing or wanting or saying. I was following my own inner compass, which seemed to be firmly set toward some as yet undiscovered area of the terrestrial globe.

My friend Marylois was one of only a few other human beings to penetrate my absorption in unhuman thoughts and goals. We met each other after she moved to Nacogdoches with her parents in 1942, and we have been close friends ever since. I have one sister born to my parents and one sister hand-picked personally by me. We were two oddballs, who found much comfort and interest in communicating with someone who was also a maverick.

We still did, after sixty years, until Alzheimer's took her away into another dimension.

Otherwise, I slid through high school as if encased in a glass bubble. Few things that other people did, said, or thought impinged upon me, for I was, as usual, busy with that inner life that has illuminated and entertained me since I can remember.

The War (WWII) came and went, and I can remember thinking how utterly stupid the entire thing was. Why should people kill or torture other people? Why should we have to go to war to stop a madman who should never have been placed in a position from which he could cause trouble? Any CHILD could have run the world better!

The War ended. High school was finished with. My teachers, with the best will in the world, urged me toward college.

There were several objections, aside from the fact that I had no desire to go. First, there was no money for college, even the local one, to which I earned scholarship money amounting, at the time, to $25.00 a term.

Secondly, I had other fish to fry. My family had built a dairy barn and converted our Grade C operation to a Grade A one, which meant electric milkers, an electric cooler, and multitudes of milk cans to wash. I had cows to milk, hay to bale, a farm to help run.

For the next ten years, in the midst of such activities, I learned to read six languages, studied everything from aardvarks to zygotes, and devoted my $30.00 a month salary to buying books. Aside from that, I learned to draw and paint, and developed a passion for opera, via radio broadcasts.

I escaped from the Conformity Machine with all working parts intact, and few of those emerging from the system can say the same. Parental support and native toughness can be credited for that, and I wish that more of both could be found in today's school systems.[4]

---

[4] Quite a lot of my children's book, *Carrots and Miggle*, derives from my own school experience and my quirky and nonconformist character. See below.

III.

MY VERY STRANGE NAME—AND NATURE

Ardath Frances Hurst Mayhar

My grandmother read Marie Corelli's novel *Ardath* around 1899. My mother was born in 1900, and she was named after the book (her cousin Coralie was named after another of Corelli's books). The copy my grandmother had was published by Hurst and Co., and the book is about a very strange poet. Twenty-four years later, my mother married a man named Hurst, and five years later gave birth to a very strange poet. As Hamlet said, "There are more things in heaven and earth, Horatio, than are dreamt of in your philosophy..."

I HAD to write fantasy, can you see that?

I am so LUCKY. My folks took me out of "the world" when I was twelve and we moved to the farm. Every one of us was vital to the functioning of the family business, and we knew it. As we got old enough to do more demanding jobs, we were automatically elevated to those. My little sister was driving the tractor, sitting on a bucket on the floor of the old Farmall so she could reach the brake, when she was four.

We all worked together in the fields, in the barns, in the hay, and everything else. Dad consulted with all of us before making a decision that committed us to something major. We were a partnership, and we shared both work and profit (when there was any), and it established a mindset that has served me well ever since.

Nothing was ever "a woman's job" or "a man's job." If there was a job to be done and I was there, I did it, whatever it might be, whether or not I was big enough to do it. That leads to great improvisation, believe me. I used to sit and think for quite a while before I began unloading twenty hundred-pound sacks of feed from the pickup, throwing them through the feed-room window, and stacking them five high. Finagling will do a lot, when sheer muscle power is lacking!

That may be why I am so impatient with what I term normal women. Often their inabilities are tied directly to the difficulty or undesirability of the task they want to avoid.

The first time someone asked me, "Are you a liberated woman?" I stared at her in shock. Liberated? From what? As with all my family, I was independent as a hog on ice.

I was young then, and my interaction with our society had just begun. My life on a dairy farm with an independent-minded and self-directed family had not prepared me for the mindsets of those shaped by a patriarchal culture.

My parents were individuals, and they conducted their lives without reference to the expectations of those around them. Their decision to move to a farm, after saving my father's pay for years, astonished even their closest friends. But that had been my father's boyhood dream, and my mother had stretched and saved his salary from the time of their marriage, in order to pay cash for land and house and barns.

He left a job that had carried them through the Depression without major problems, but security was never their first priority. We moved, started a dairy, and as a child I was a valued partner in making our living. My brother, my younger sister, and I worked in the dairy and in the fields. This was no terrible hardship (although I must admit that I would have preferred to be left alone to read), for my father told wonderful stories, we laughed and joked, and the time in the fields was no big deal.

By the time I graduated from high school we were building a Grade A dairy barn. This meant that we used milking machines, rather than our long-suffering hands, to milk the cows. For three hundred sixty-five days a year we milked those cows, ranging from twenty-five to thirty in number, baled hay for them, fertilized pasture, built fences, distributed the hay in winter. Our income depended upon that work, and we all knew ourselves to be important elements in our survival as a family.

My father and mother expected each of us to do whatever was necessary, whatever the situation and whether or not there was assistance at hand. We did. It never occurred to me that there was anything I was incapable of doing or that anything was doable only by a man.

A major heart attack when I was nineteen put my father out of commission for the better part of a year. My brother was still in high school, and my sister was only a child, but my mother and I did the work without thinking twice about it. You had to be in the right place at the right time, or one cow or another would either kick you into the middle of next week or cover you with manure, both excellent motivations for staying on schedule. Given the nature of publishing, this was invaluable training.

I used to drive the pickup to town, buy twenty hundred-pound bags of cow feed, drive home, unload those bags into the feed room of the barn, then stack them five-high. As I stood at five feet two inches and weighed about a hundred twenty pounds at the time, I did a lot of figuring and maneuvering, but those bags got stacked.

As long as I was undamaged physically, I would tackle any job of any size, and usually I conquered it. At no time in my growing up was I ever told that because I was a girl or because I was small or because of anything else, I couldn't accomplish what was necessary. It is that sort of verbal conditioning, more than any other element, that makes too many people victims of the system.

Of course, today's educational system adds its own impact, but when I was in school in the Thirties and Forties schools did their job as to teaching students to think and to find out what they needed to know. Though Nacogdoches, Texas, was a small town—about 5,000 population—its schools provided excellent grounding in the basics, plus art and music.

When I graduated in 1947, I was able to find out anything I desired to know without attending the local teacher's college. That summer I helped my family build our Grade A dairy barn, while helping with milking the cows, working in the fields, and doing anything else that came to hand. When my father had his first heart attack, I took over running the dairy.

For several years I kept on with that without any break, until my best friend, Marylois Dunn, hauled me off to my first writer's conference in Corpus Christi, Texas, in 1952. I was becoming a hermit, and she recognized that and did something about it in her usual decisive manner. For several years, we attended the Southwest Writer's Conference there, and this was what "education" I had in writing. As this included association with and talks by people like J. Frank Dobie, Fred Gipson, Harrison Smith (the editor of the *Saturday Review of Literature*), and professional writers from all over the country, it was an enviable one.

But what other education did I pursue? Well, farming gives one plenty of time to think. While shoveling manure, milking cows, building fence, the hands are busy, but—that work does not demand full attention. I wrote poetry while I worked, and in winter and between busy times I studied.

Classical Greek, Latin, French, Spanish, German, and Italian were among the languages I tackled and learned to read with varying degrees of proficiency. Interested in everything imaginable, I delved into ancient and medieval history, archeology, anthropology, philosophy, theology, the physical sciences, mathematical concepts (though I hated the applications), literature, poetics, and just about everything else. Having a mind that retains almost everything I encounter, this intensive study has been incredibly helpful to me as a writer. Seldom do I have to do in-depth research, except for occasional specifics, when writing historical or military material. The basic information seems to be in place.

I also believe that I have lived many incarnations as everything from a Greek hoplite to an Anasazi healer. I can remember things that it is impossible I should ever have encountered in this present life.

Also when I was nineteen, Ayn Rand's *The Fountainhead* was published. I ordered a copy of the book after reading a review in *Saturday Review of Literature,* and it probably is one of the reasons that I am the person I am today. It taught me to look closely at truisms handed out by the Establishment and never to accept, unquestioned, anything people in power proclaim.

Then a few years later I ordered, after reading a review in the *Houston Post,* Charles Williams's *The Place of the Lion,* which is metaphysical, scholarly, and fascinating. This was the book that showed me that you can mix ideas that matter greatly to you in a philosophical vein with action, adventure, and good storytelling. Probably those two books had the greatest impact upon my work of any I have ever read except possibly the original *Adventures in Time and Space.*

IV.

SERPENTS

In East Texas we have every variety of poisonous snake in North America. Sensible parents ignore politically correct behavior and teach toddlers prejudice against serpents as soon as possible, when they live in the country or even very small towns where a brightly striped coral snake may be lying innocently along the foundation or under a bush.

With water moccasins, copperheads, coral snakes, and rattlesnakes likely to appear in yards and gardens, fields, and barn lots, making your child fearful enough to run when he sees a long and legless shape in the grass is better than having him or her reach down to pick it up. Many youngsters have died of snakebite in this part of the world, simply because they were fearless.

As we lived as much of our lives at the cabin as possible, with two ponds full of moccasins at our doorstep, that instilled fear was a precaution that probably saved the lives of my brother and me many times. To this day I "never see this fellow, attended or alone, without a tighter breathing and zero at the bone," as Emily Dickinson put it. My first snake encounter must have happened when I was about three. If that green snake, twined around a young pine, had been a boa constrictor, it couldn't have frightened me more.

I tried to pick him, thinking he was an intriguingly smooth green vine, as he coiled up the slender trunk of a pine sapling. When my gaze slid down that spiral to find a narrow head flicking its tongue at me, my heart just about stopped. I can still feel that moment of gut-wrenching terror, though I have to some extent conquered my life-long phobia. Now if snakes leave me alone, I leave them alone.

The fish-ponds at the cabin hatched water moccasins as if they'd been intended for that purpose. The smaller pond lay some forty or fifty feet from the porch of the cabin, divided by a dam from the big pond downstream. Willows leaned over the dam, pines fringed the banks, and the shallow edges of the water made perfect moccasin breeding country amid the pond moss growing in the mud of the bottom.

We had a small pier built out over the pond closest to the cabin, from which we could fish. Beside that was a clump of willows rising out of the water. To one of them Dad fastened the live box, where we kept minnows for fish bait. This was a wooden crate some three feet by three, with a hardware-cloth bottom to let the water circulate. It lay half in and half out of the water, convenient for pulling out when we needed more minnows.

We pulled it onto the bank in the fall, but usually the water in the pond rose to sink it partially before spring came again. One day my granddad, my brother, and I were walking along the bank, checking out the spring and thinking of good times to come. Daddy Joe had his Colt .45 revolver at his belt, as usual. He sat on the stump of a big oak that had died and been felled. "Go pull the live box up farther," he told us, and we waded out and heaved on the cord.

The box rolled to one side, and a dozen or more cottonmouth moccasins rose from the mud beneath it, their wicked white mouths looking like a garden of fanged flowers on long mud-colored stems. Buzz leaped in one direction, I leaped in the other, and Daddy Joe's pistol went off with a huge explosion. Bits of snake and mud and water went everywhere. A hole appeared in the mud, and the tea-colored water trickled into it to mix with the blood of the snakes.

I have used those moccasins many times in my writing. That picture is etched into my mind in living color. A writer, be it known, wastes nothing.

Daddy Joe had his own snake experiences, but the one I recall best involves his china nest-egg. He'd wanted one for years, but he was stingy with himself and wouldn't invest in it. Finally somebody gave him a beautiful white one, and he gleefully put it into one of the nests in the hay barn. For a week we gathered eggs, and the china egg was there, shining milky white in the dim light. Then it was gone, obviously swallowed by a chicken snake.

Though he griped a bit, it was no big deal. A year later, we were moving along the bank of the big creek behind the barn when we came upon a big fat chicken snake lying along the path. Daddy Joe killed him with a stick and said, "Look! He's just swallowed one of my eggs."

Sure enough, there was a large lump in his middle. When my granddad tried with his heavy boot to push it up to his mouth, it wouldn't budge, though usually that was an easy task. He went after the axe, and when he cut the serpent open there was his china egg, encysted.

I have often thought of the puzzlement and discomfort of that snake after he swallowed that "egg" and then couldn't break and digest it. It actually grew into a sort of pocket inside him, secured by muscle and tissue.

Daddy Joe washed the egg in the creek, put it back into the nest, and the next week it was gone again. Some other unfortunate chicken snake probably died with it embedded in his gut. Somewhere amid the fields and pastures of the old farm, a china egg still lies hidden.

* * * * * * *

There was no way to roam the farm or use the boat on the pond without meeting water moccasins. My brother and I were about five and eight when we went with Daddy Joe to run set-lines in the big pond. Willows grew out in the water, and where old clumps had died there were forests of low snags sticking out.

As we passed a group of snags, my granddad suddenly began hitting something with his paddle. After a minute, he reached forward and poked again. A moccasin was sticking his head over the side of the boat, time after time as he worked his way along it, trying to slide over the edge. Daddy Joe fought him up and down the side and back of the boat for what seemed like hours, before he finally discouraged the creature enough to allow him to use the paddle to get us out of there. We probably broke all records for speed attained by a flat-bottomed fishing boat propelled by a single paddle.

We were in the deepest part of the pond, but if that moccasin had succeeded in boarding our boat, we'd all have abandoned ship without hesitation. A water moccasin has a nasty temper at best, and after being repelled with a boat paddle he had to have felt even uglier than usual.

It wasn't just at the cabin that snakes posed a problem, though. We lived in town at that time, on the edge of Nacogdoches, Texas, which was a town of about 5,000. Coach-whips and chicken snakes were the serpents usually found in our neighborhood, and several times we found one of our cats dabbing cautiously at one, fascinated but repulsed.

The worst instance involved some neighbors, however. A group of children located a coach-whip in front of our house. A particularly boastful and unintelligent fellow who lived at the bottom of the hill came along, stopped his car, and got out to examine the find. Being one of those idiots, he caught up the snake and cracked it like a whip to snap its head off. But his hand slipped, and the snake wrapped around the neck of a small girl who was watching.

She promptly went into hysterics. These days he'd have been sued for everything down to his fillings and his boot heels, but then he just got the snake off and went about his business.

I never learned, after we moved away, if the little girl recovered her nerve. I don't guarantee that I would have.

I farmed for ten years without having a serious run-in with a snake, and when my husband and I moved to Oregon in 1968 we moved out of bad snake country. Western Oregon's waters are too cold for water snakes, but even a devoted rock-hunter, which I was, had been so conditioned never to put my hand into a hole in a creek bank that it took me years to be able to do that without a shiver.

V.

THE CABIN

I have been accused of lying about the earliest things I can remember by those whose childhood memories begin somewhere about the age of four or five. Still, I can see clear, colored, moving pictures of things that took place when I was little more than two years old.

I have a vivid imagination, but even that could not explain the fact that I could build a log cabin and a pole-and-cat chimney right now, though the only time that has ever taken place around me was the summer after I was two. The techniques used in 1932 are probably long lost by now.

My parents and grandparents decided to build a log cabin on my granddad's farm near Timpson, Texas. They'd dug two big fish ponds along a creek in a pine wood, and on the bank of the smaller one they laid out the twenty-foot square that was to become THE CABIN. It always appears in my mind in capitals.

I watched sweaty black carpenters put together a big square of peeled pine logs, climbing higher and higher up the closed "pen" as the walls grew. From my two and a half-foot elevation, it looked as if it went up into the sky. But that was only the beginning.

The roof went on, and I don't remember what it was made of, because I was entirely too short to see. Probably tin, for that has always been a favorite roofing material in the south. I've seen old houses sink to the ground, still carrying rusty tin roofs that persistently kept out water. But it might have been pine shingles.

Then the fun started. Playing with mud is any child's delight, and the spaces between the logs had to be chinked with pats of yellow-clay mud mixed with straw and water. Though I wasn't allowed to "play" with the builders, it was fun to watch, as their dark skins became smeared with yellow-gray streaks, and their hair turned into sculpted spikes as dabs dropped onto them from above.

Best of all was building the chimney, which was done the old way, by constructing a frame of poles and then filling it in around the central opening with "cats," which were more handfuls of clay mud and straw, shaped and smoothed into place. The straw stuck out randomly, like whiskers, and the clay felt, to my probing fingers, very powdery when it dried. That yellowish soil had a unique, acrid smell that still means summer to me when I happen on a patch of it, dried to dust in August. A very old black man named Puckett was the chimney builder, being the only person around who remembered that almost forgotten method of construction. I'm surprised that I remember that name...I hadn't thought of him in sixty years.

Later that fall, I helped my Dad "paper" the ceiling with long rolls of brown paper. My job was to stick upholstery tacks through squares of cardboard that he tacked up at regular intervals to keep the long swaths from sagging. Though the cardboard was thin and the tacks sharp, my small fingers found it a demanding task. Thirty-odd years later, the last time I saw The Cabin, that paper and those squares were still there, doing their job. Not until later did I realize why my mother wasn't helping us. The next February my younger brother was born, and she certainly didn't need to be climbing up and down ladders.

The cardboard, I remember quite clearly, was formed of the backs of "snuff books." No, nothing to do with snuff films—my Dad sold Levi Garrett snuff for the American Tobacco Company, and one of their advertising pieces was a little memo book with advertising on the cover, jokes on alternate pages, and lined pages for notes and addresses. We cut those into one-inch squares; long years later when the Cabin burned, those ancient jokes were still attached to that faded brown paper ceiling.

Later that fall we camped in the still windowless space, which had rectangular holes for front and back doors. Dad and Mr. Mack, his good friend, sawed out (with hand-saws) more rectangles for windows. It was tough work, for the logs were about eight inches in diameter, and sawing a hole some two feet by four raised blisters, sweat, and some grumbling, although neither Mr. Mack nor my Dad was a cussing kind of man.

Then Dad, who was a neat and accurate builder and cabinet maker, made thick shutters that fastened inside with wooden pegs that fitted into hasps. During the long weeks in winter when we couldn't get there because of flooding or terribly slick mud roads, the shutters kept vandals from going in and tearing up our small private version of heaven. Ironically, it was vandals, probably from the same family that posed the threat in the beginning,[5] who burned the place at last, some time in the 1970s.

That first winter we visited the cabin on weekends, when we could negotiate the slick, yellow clay roads, building great fires in the big fireplace and cooking on the cast iron wood-burning cook stove. That was long before the days of rural electrification, and we used coal-oil lamps for light. Those hung on the wall in black metal holders with silvery reflectors to multiply the effect of the mellow light.

The furnishings were simple but sufficient. Dad built bunks against the wall; those could be folded up out of the way when not in use. There was a double bed for him and Mem, a green-enameled table, and he built two benches that fitted on each side of the table. Those benches were still in use for years in my sister's home, and a lot of grandchildren and great-grandchildren have sat on them in the past decades.

The flying squirrels that lived in the huge pine tree against the west wall invaded the attic, finding it a snug winter home. Later they came down into the cabin itself. One summer when I was about seven or eight, we arrived for our summer-long sojourn. Mem opened the silverware drawer in the old-fashioned screen-fronted dish safe to find a row of tiny eyes staring at her among the knives and forks.

When she unrolled the bunk mattresses, four more small furry shapes appeared in the middle of the roll on the top bunk. Charming as they were, the little rodents were as

---

[5] They showed up, somewhat disguised, in my novel, *The World Ends in Hickory Hollow*.

destructive as mice. For that reason, Dad decided to hunt them out of the attic, stationing my brother and me with our new Christmas B-B guns, to shoot them as the emerged from the rafters. Our tomcat Smudge entered into the game with gusto, until a rodent bit him entirely through the end of his nose. After that one could walk over him and he wouldn't stir.

* * * * * * *

The summer I was three, I caught my first big fish. Big for a three-year-old, anyway. Dad was sitting on a cot under the pines, tending to my infant brother. I was standing on the bank of the pond, holding Dad's long bamboo fish pole. Suddenly something hit the bait, and I found myself being pulled into the pond.

It never occurred to me to turn loose. To this day, I'm worse than a snapping turtle—I don't even turn loose when it thunders. So I went into that muddy-edged pond, to knees, to waist, before Dad could reach me and take hold of my hands (he didn't take that pole away from me, being much the same sort of person I am). Together, we backed out of the pond with a two-pound large-mouth bass in tow.

I don't know if I caught the fish or the bass caught me. But that was my first fish and I'll never forget that sunny, hot day under the resiny smelling pines, holding the pole while I watched carefully to make sure no water moccasin was creeping up on my bare toes. The ponds could have been dug as water-moccasin hatcheries, for that was their main output, and it must have been real fun to keep an eye on toddlers there.

A couple of years later, the worst almost happened. It was another hot East Texas summer. My Dad and I were fishing on the bank where I caught that first fish, beside a bit of lattice on which we used to lay poles and bait. I watched my bit of dried pine twig that served as a bobber, so concentrated that I wouldn't have seen a dinosaur if it had approached.

Suddenly I found myself in mid-air, only recalling in hindsight the grip of strong hands that sent me sailing some ten or twelve feet onto the sloping bank behind us. Before I could wonder just what was happening, I hit hard, rolled, and saw my Dad killing a snake with the stick that we never went without in summer.

A cottonmouth moccasin had been lying alongside the lattice, having been wounded, and crawled up on land, sick. Its head was about an inch from my foot, Dad said. He saw, he leaped, and he tossed me clear almost before he had time to think. An old moccasin has enough venom to kill a small child, and that one was big and fat and ugly.

That is why country people always taught their children, with great care and persistence, to be afraid of snakes. Here we have every kind of poisonous snake in the continental U.S.

It was about then that my brother and I learned to swim. Anyone who remembers water-wings reveals his/her age. This was before plastic or even rubber float toys. The "wings" were made of canvas coated with something odd and stiff. You had to wet the wings and then blow them up until they inflated into a pair of small blobs that were attached by a strip across the chest. Supported so, I found myself able to paddle around in the ponds, under the eyes of mother, grandmother, or Dad.

My granddad, Daddy Joe, was the perfect grandfather, but he never grew up to be more than ten years old, though he was superbly competent at his job and was incredibly bright. Maybe that was WHY he was such a great grandfather. What we didn't think of, he most certainly would. How my parents dared to turn the three of us loose together I cannot, at this point, imagine, even though I tended to stop "growing up" at the age of ten, too.

As Dad traveled for the snuff company five and a half days a week, in summer he and Mem would load two children, two or three cats, a couple of bird dogs (sometimes a litter of pups, too) into my mother's 1935 Plymouth. He would take his company Chevy, and we would all head for the farm. We stopped for fresh bread (several loaves) and ice for the ice box on the way.

We'd spend that first weekend together, getting the fishing gear into order, digging out the ancient woolen bathing suits with knee-length legs and elbow-length arms, seining for minnows to keep in the live-box, and drawing out the well.

What? I can hear running-water people wondering. When a well remains unused for some time, all sorts of impurities can get into it, from frogs and dead plants to mosquito larvae. So you draw all the water out of the well and let it fill again, the deep pure spring providing clean drinking water in abundance.

Dad built a cement floor beside the well, set posts into it, and hung tow feed bags around the sides to make a place for baths. We'd draw the bath water early in the afternoon and let it sit in the number three washtubs to warm in the sun. Then we'd take turns washing with soap and warm water, standing on the slippery cement, and then rinsing with the icy water freshly drawn in the long narrow well bucket.

One evening my aunt slipped on the cement and splashed bottom-first into the tub of water. We had two grown English setters and about five pups at that time. They all ran pell-mell into the bathing enclosure to see what was happening, and every time she would almost get her feet under her they pushed her back into the tub, while she shouted for help. At last Uncle Raymond, her husband, overcame his laughter enough to rescue her from her would-be rescuers.

* * * * * * *

My grandmother was a crack shot with my Granddad's Colt revolver, a hog-leg that I couldn't lift until I was about ten years old. She also rode sidesaddle the most spirited black horse in that end of the county. Indeed, when my mother was an infant in 1900, my grandmother put her in the buggy, hitched up that black horse, and drove thirty miles to visit her mother, through real wilderness that was alive with bears, cougars, bobcats, and two-legged predators.

When she wanted to visit her mother she went, an all-day journey, with that revolver in her lap and Mem in a basket at her feet. She never had to shoot anybody, but everyone in the county understood that "Miss Julia" wouldn't hesitate to blow them away, if they threatened her and her baby. Being out in the woods miles from town and totally out of sight and earshot from the nearest farm held no terrors for her or my mother, so we children never had it occur to us that there was anything on earth to fear.

When we reached the first "gap" (literally a gap in the fence closed with a wire section that folded back), they'd turn me, my brother, the dogs, and the cats out to run and shout and leap and chortle like wild things the mile or so through the woods to the cabin. And thereafter, once we were about three and six, we had the run of the two hundred-fifty-acre farm, alone or together or with Whiz and Stubby, the setter dogs.

Once we happened on a man stealing pine poles and loading them into his wagon. Knowing no fear, I asked him, "What are you doing with Daddy Joe's trees?"

Only later did I realize the reason why he leaped into the wagon and drove away: I held on a double lead both setters, and Whiz, who did not like black people, was baring his teeth and raising his hackles. When I understood that it was not this fierce six-year-old who frightened off the timber thief, I was considerably disappointed.

We roamed from the woods around the cabin to the pastures around the big hay and cattle barns and beyond, across the deep creek where we fished for crawfish and gathered pawpaws, to the distant wood where Daddy Joe killed the red fox that had been getting his chickens. Taking a bucket, a couple of lengths of string, and some fat bacon, we'd visit the deep hole in that far creek when we had a craving to get crawfish.

Squatting on the muddy gravel, we'd tie a bit of fat to a string and let it down into one of the crawfish holes, which were topped by neat towers of mud. After a while (a pretty short while, actually) we'd pull up sharply, and often a startled crawfish would be lifted into the light and fall on dry ground, jerked out of his tower. Those went into the bucket to be used for fish bait later when the family fished for bass and white perch.

Summer was heaven: the woods, the ponds, the creeks, the frogs singing in the evening, first the high-pitched ones crying "Knee-deep! Knee-deep!" Then the middle-sized ones calling "Hip-deep! Hip-deep!" and last the big old buster frogs rumbling "Belly-deep! Belly-deep!"

Long days were spent rambling through the resiny pines and the powdery yellow dust, digging worms that were a foot long in some places, and fishing with them for sun perch in the edges of the big ponds.

When we were very small, we were put down for naps on the porch of the cabin, on canvas and wood cots. Some time in the middle of the afternoons the cow across the pond on the neighbor's place would come down to the water to drink, her bell clanking with a mellow sadness that still, when something catches that timbre, brings back the smells of powdery soil and murky water and the feel of unbleached domestic sheet under my childish cheek.

It was the sort of memory that every child should have; for as long as I live the cabin will offer me a haven of peace and joy, no matter what is happening in my present.[6]

---

[6]Many elements in my children's book, *The Dropouts*, had their origin in this part of my life.

VI.

THE FARM/DAIRY

1942-1957

I used to rake hay with a mule-drawn hay rake made for a tall man to operate. I'd pull up a batch in line with the windrow, stop the mule, climb down off the high metal seat to trip the release and raise the rake, cluck to the mule, who would move forward enough to clear the windrow, then climb up again and make another round. Our mule was something of a genius—he caught on very quickly, and would turn his head to watch and then move up as soon as the rake was clear; we worked out a pretty fast and efficient method, considering the problems.

He also taught me to plow. When I was tall enough to reach the plow handles, Dad told me to plow between the rows of young corn. I clucked to old Sam and off we went. At the end of the row was the edge of the woods, and I was beginning to wonder just how to go about turning to catch the next row. Before I could finish figuring, Sam turned his neck to see past the blinder on his halter and gave me a LOOK.

"You gump," it said. "Pick up the plow out of the ground."

So I picked up the plow, Sam walked forward into the trees, swung around neatly and started down the row to the left. Once he got lined up I set the plow again and off we went. Dad didn't tell me. He knew Sam would educate me, and he did. That mule had more sense than a lot of people I have known since.

Farming allows a wonderful scope for thinking. While the hands are busy with tasks they can do on automatic, the mind can fly free. I wrote much poetry while milking cows or distributing hay or hoeing corn, and, later in my life, I did my best philosophical essays while ironing clothes.

Because of this intellectual freedom and the availability of books and magazines, my years on the farm were in many ways far more educational than an equal amount of time spent in a college or university. This method of self-education would not have worked for anyone who was not self-disciplined and motivated, but it worked beautifully for me.[7]

---

[7] All the technical stuff, plus the wolves and the tornado from *Carrots and Miggle*, came from these years.

VII.

TAKING OFF

From early childhood I was fascinated by airplanes. When one flew over the house in town and later over the farm, I would dash out, if possible, to watch it until it disappeared over the horizon. At last, when I was perhaps thirteen or fourteen, Dad took the family to the airport at Nacogdoches.

The manager there, who also taught flying, was a friend of his and my grandfather's, and he took me and my sister up in a small plane. I was hooked! But this was during the war, and there was neither fuel nor money to spend on learning to fly. That had to wait for years.

When I bought my first bookstore in 1957 I met a number of people I would not otherwise have known. One couple I met both flew, and after a time they began to take me out to the airfield on Sundays. Mr. Terry, who still ran the place, agreed to teach me to fly for a sum I could manage, and we began. We practiced stalls, climbed over the clouds, practiced emergency landings over the river bottom pastures, where we frightened a lot of cows with our touch-and-go intrusions.

For all his skill as a pilot, Mr. Terry was not an articulate man. I am one who needs to have things explained in words. This made learning to land very difficult for me, as he expected me to duplicate his actions, and without knowing what they were and why I found it frustrating. At last a commercial pilot who flew for a local corporation came in one Sunday, listened to the tale of our difficulties, and volunteered to go around with me for some touch-and-go landings.

He talked me through two without a hitch. Then he got out and said, "You can do it now. Go ahead and solo." And I did, flawlessly.

I drove home that night filled with glee. Coming in the back door through my Dad's room, I found him already in bed. "I soloed!" I chortled.

He turned pale. That was two shocks he had that day, for earlier my young sister had told him she wanted to marry her beau. She was sixteen and her husband to be was nineteen. Dad was crazy about Don, so they married, and it was one of those things that was a perfect match. They are still going strong after more than fifty years.

Luckily Dad survived the double whammy, but I would have spared him the news about soloing if I had known what had gone before.

Several months afterward Joe and I married, and I never had the money to fly again. But I learned how, and I wouldn't take anything for having accomplished that. It has come in useful for several stories and at least one book, for there are things about flying a small craft that are not mentioned in books about flying—that funny wobble that comes at the point when you need to pull up the nose to land, for instance. That happens when you are very close to the ground and the aerodynamic effect is interrupted by the soil below.

Nothing I ever did has been wasted, I am pretty certain.[8]

---

[8] A bit at the beginning of *Medicine Walk* derived from my time in a small plane.

VIII.

WOLVES AND A TORNADO

The inexorable thing about a dairy is that the cows MUST be milked twice a day. A cow running with her calf at her side is in good shape—he suckles often, keeping the pressure off her udder. A dairy cow, however, is bred to give far more milk than the natural system needs, and she can only be relieved by being milked. Whether the lights go off, the cows refuse to cooperate, whatever, this must be done or expensive animals can be ruined.

Early in our Grade A dairy career (about 1948), on a gray January afternoon that turned into a pitch-dark night, we were milking along when suddenly the barn filled with dead leaves and sweetgum balls. The big back doors bowed inward, and the noise was such that nothing could be heard except the drum of stuff against the walls and the roof. For a wonder, the lights didn't go off, which they tended to do if even a big cloud came up, so we kept right on going. My sister (about six or seven at the time) we put into the feed room, which was finished in thick planks. Once I looked up from putting a milker on a cow, and she was looking around the animal's rear end, eyes wide. "It surely is blowing hard!" she shouted.

About the time the worst of the noise subsided, the back door slid aside and my brother appeared, drenched and upset. "Dad, the corner has blown off the barn roof and all our hay's getting wet," he said. Without a word, Dad handed me the strip bucket and set off to rescue that hay, which we had sweated and labored to bale the summer before. Judy, my sister, began bringing feed, letting out the cows we had finished with and letting in the next pair. Together we finished up the last dozen or so cows, and cleaned up the equipment and the barn. Still no flicker of the lights.

When we looked out of the back door, we found to our dismay that the calf shed some yards from the dairy barn was gone, along with the calf that had been inside it. We later found the calf, somewhat sore and lame but alive, two lots east of the barn lot, and bits of the shed as well. Besides that, the tornado tore off the southeast corner of the hay barn roof and completely demolished the "pig palace" in the hog pasture, though the sow was unharmed.

It also destroyed the Appleby, Texas, post office and a church there, as well as raking a path through the pine woods and tearing up houses as it came across them. We were lucky to get off as lightly as we did—and that the electricity didn't go out.

A few years later, one summer evening, we called the cows and they didn't come at once, as they usually did. When Dad went to find them, they came in a rush, running as if they had gone mad, which they had. The pack of southern red wolves that laired on the next farm was changing its location and their smell got to the herd. When that happened, they went wild, running over or through anything that got in their way, eyes rolled back, streaming green manure until they looked as if they'd been painted green. This was the worst "spell of wolves" we ever had to deal with.

We had to rope individual cows and haul them into the barn, hose them off, and sterilize their udders before we could milk them. Instead of being through at seven, as we ordinarily were, we finished up some time between ten and eleven. By that time we were as messy and mad and walleyed as the cows, too.

IX.

CONTEXT SHAPES THE WRITER

I have taught my students for many years that the setting of a story can shape plot and action in dramatic ways. Only relatively recently have I begun to realize how deeply we are shaped by the places where we grew up or lived in for long periods of time. Geography is so vital and omnipresent in our lives that we tend to be unconscious of it, until we look back from adulthood.

The way we speak is often formed or at least influenced by our place of birth. Yet even more inherent in our makeup are the mindsets that we accepted as the norm as we grew up. Often we do not recognize the reality of our home country until we move away and see it from afar.

Living in Oregon for many years, I looked back at East Texas and the upbringing it allowed me, and began to realize how unique and valuable it was. Not for amenities—those were not a part of this area in the 1930s—but for the focus on honest dealing, truthfulness, and self-reliance that I had thought must be inherent in any place. There is room here for eccentricity, for independence of mind and of lifestyle, and for divergence from the popular attitudes that make up political correctness and other such dogmas. Also, unfortunately, for all kinds of personal and political bigotry or chicanery, but that is probably true everywhere.

There was elbow room to grow in unusual ways. Armed with sticks, my brother and I would "Injun" through the pine woods or ramble along the creeks or dig for worms and fish, on our own, until our growling bellies reminded us of mealtime.

Muddy or dusty, depending on the season, we would return to the cabin that was our camp-house beside the fish ponds. We'd draw water from the well in the conical bucket with the twisty handle, wash up in an enamel bowl using Ivory soap, and scoot onto the long bench beside the table, indoors in winter, outdoors in summer, waiting for fried catfish or bass, hot biscuits, corn on the cob, fresh field peas—whatever bounty the generous land provided.

We were too young to know that in other places beyond the seas there were people starving, being driven from their homes by power-mad rulers bent on world domination. If we had known it would have worried us greatly, for we had learned by example from our parents and grandparents that we could always spare something for those in need. That was an East Texas trait, even in the depths of the Depression.

X.

BACKING INTO MARRIAGE

1957

When I was a child it always puzzled me when other little girls would say, "When-I-grow-up-'n'-get-married," all one word, without a whisper of a doubt that this was the only goal in life. That was never any aim of mine, as I lived a rich life in my imagination, dealing with the world of reality capably but without paying it much attention.

Growing up on the farm, I was insulated from the world of the 1940s and '50s and its attitudes. Given the nature of my family, I had never considered what others thought or did, as long as it didn't impinge on my life and work. That changed in 1957. I found it impossible to work with my brother when he returned from military service to operate the dairy farm. He intended to be Sarge and for me to be Beetle Bailey. As you might guess, that did not go down well with me. After a particularly infuriating confrontation, I received a call from a "shirt-tail cousin" in Nacogdoches. Miss Vera owned a bookstore, and she had reached the point at which she wanted to sell out and move to Dallas to be near her daughter.

A bookstore was my natural habitat, as much as the woods were. I went to my Dad and asked him for the down payment. I had worked for ten years, several of those without pay and the rest at thirty dollars a month. I thought I had accrued some credit in the family account, and he agreed. So I bought East Texas Bookstore and settled in to run it.

Around the corner was a taxi stand, and driving a cab there was Joe Earl Mayhar, a bookaholic of the first water. If I had set a trap, I couldn't have been more successful at hauling him in, though that was no part of my thinking at all.

Joe was divorced, the father of two small sons. Robert, the older, lived with Joe's aunt and uncle; William lived with Joe's parents. Joe had no intention of forming entangling alliances, any more than I did. But he was a science fiction fan of long standing, and I was the last in a chain of readers who passed along sf paperbacks. Once he found he could borrow sf books from me, he was a constant visitor to the shop.

After a while it became clear that we enjoyed talking with each other a great deal. He would come in during his lunch hour, and we would discuss everything under the sun, including books we'd read. I lived pretty far out in the country, and Joe had no car of his own at that time, so we didn't consider anything as *outré* as a date, until we had come to realize that we truly liked each other a LOT.

We had exactly one date (the only one I ever had with anyone), for which Joe borrowed his brother-in-law's car. Wouldn't you know—that evening it rained like crazy, and our mud road was both slick and treacherous. But we went to a movie (sf of course) and made it back unscathed. Not long afterward Joe got permission to drive his cab out to see me one Sunday and I showed him my favorite parts of the woods. Sitting on a log beside the creek, we agreed that we would get married.

In June of 1957 we were married in my mother's living room and moved into an apartment on Hospital Street in Nacogdoches, in walking distance of the store. Joe went to business college in the morning and drove the cab in the afternoon for some time. Let me here testify that marrying at age twenty-eight, after a lifetime of hard physical work, makes the wedding night a very painful thing. But we both survived.

We were married for forty-one years, until Joe's death in 1999.

I still miss him.

XI.

JOE

My husband was a strange man, the product of a horribly difficult and damaging upbringing. Though his father, as a veteran of WWI, had received the same separation bonus others did and bought with it a small farm, with mules and a cow, he was no manager. Even raising chickens, pigs, and having the Davy Crockett National Forest, full of game, adjacent to his land, his children were consistently ill-fed. In a few years he had lost the land, starved his livestock, and was farming on the halves, the bottom of8 the food chain for a farmer. Often Joe went to school barefoot in mid-winter. He had pneumonia almost every winter.

Not only that, both his parents were angry people, and Joe seemed to get the brunt of their cruel impulses. He was an oddball, and his father was determined to make him into a sort of serf, bound to serve the family without pay. This resulted in the boy's leaving home at fifteen.

Joe was extremely intelligent, reading everything available, wherever he was. He reinvented himself, when he found that he did not know ordinary usages of polite society. By the time we met in 1957, he had done a creditable job on himself.

Nevertheless, he was a difficult person to live with, though he could be loving and generous to a fault. In light of present knowledge, I have decided that he, and probably his father before him, suffered from clinical depression on a recurring basis. Indeed, two of his sons have the same problem. Over forty-one years I learned to cope with his moods without committing either homicide or divorce, and all in all it was worth it.

He could learn anything he wanted to, and over the course of his life he became a competent mechanic, an excellent salesman, a fair electrician and plumber—and he taught himself to use, repair, and teach others to use computers. He would give you the shirt off his back, but if you tried to take it by force you were in for a real fight.

I cannot imagine anyone who could have lived with me for that length of time without killing me, and I feel that no one less tenacious than I would have stuck with him through thick and thin. It was a case of two weirdoes creating a satisfactory life together instead of ruining the lives of two innocent bystanders.

There are worse ways to live.

XII.

OUR OWN OREGON TRAIL

1968

The Oregon Trail has more than historical meaning for me and my family. In the Sixties, for many reasons, my husband Joe and I decided to move away from Texas, and after subscribing for a year to the newspaper published in Corvallis, Oregon, we began making preparations for the move.

We had very little money. After looking around carefully for the best way in which to transport household furnishings, thousands of pounds of books, two adults, a teenager, and two young children across two-thirds of the continent, we purchased a forty-eight-passenger school bus and stripped out all except the front row of seats.

While waiting for our home to be sold, we packed into that space my grandmother's upright piano (made in 1902), other furniture, boxes and boxes of books, dishes, cookware, clothing, etc. When we weighed bus and all on the public scales, the entire equipage totaled sixteen thousand pounds.

Behind the bus we towed our Chevrolet van, which was also loaded with luggage for the trip, plus odds and ends that would not fit into the bus. In July of 1968 we completed the sale of our home (we had a couple of thousand dollars left after paying off the mortgage and setting aside enough money for the trip), and set out.

School buses have governors on them: forty-five miles an hour was just about our best speed. The weight was such that we had no jack capable of lifting the bus, should we have a flat. But we were relatively young, filled with energy and excitement, and we knew we'd make it to our destination, whatever problems arose along the way.

The first day we stopped at a park in order to retrieve something from the van. As we pulled into the drive, from the other end another vehicle pulled in. In it were the father and two children of good friends who had been living in Florida for several years. We sat on a low stone wall and had a final visit with them—truly a final visit. The next year both those children died in a traffic accident.

We covered about seventy miles that first day, stopping in Tyler, Texas, to fill up with gas and find a motel for the night. As we sat in front of the gas station, one of the dual tires on the bus went flat. The station had a tire to fit, but we had to go downtown to find a tube for it.

In Tyler lived the parents of close friends who had just moved back from Hawaii. We tried to phone them, but their number was unlisted. As we sat in front of the tire store, Joe told me and the boys, "You watch that intersection. Our friends are going to come along and stop at the red light. When they do, run out and stop them."

They did. We did. That night we had a farewell visit with them as well, and it was several years before we saw them again.

It took us three days to get out of Texas, at the rate we had to travel and with the weight we had to move. We spent the third night in Dumas, Texas, after having our second flat just outside town. That one got fixed, too, without any problem.

The fourth night we spent in Pueblo, Colorado, amid a pounding rainstorm. The next morning we set out toward Monarch Pass. At that time carburetors were not fuel-injected. They were set to handle the air-gasoline mixture at whatever altitude they were to work. The mix was not sufficient to get sixteen thousand pounds up to almost fourteen thousand feet.

Even the van, detached from the bus, wouldn't make the climb. We had to be towed to the top (there were businesses halfway up the pass for just that purpose). Going down was an adventure all its own. Luckily Joe had, in his youth, been a truck driver and knew to go down in the same gear required to go up a grade, so we didn't burn out our brakes or lose control.

We stopped at the bottom, thoroughly wrung out, to find that the man at the station there had just gassed up a car from Texas belonging to people we knew. He looked up the credit card slip, those being more leisurely and personally interested times. Things were beginning to look a bit strange, at that point, though as yet we didn't understand quite how strange they were to become.

We, being lowlanders, felt that had to be the worst climb we would meet along the way. After all, it was the Continental Divide, wasn't it?

Wrong! After Monarch came Blue Mesa. Even now it is a tough pull, but thirty-odd years ago it was incredibly more difficult. The grades were much steeper going up, and the two-lane highway was a series of switchbacks going down at a perilous angle. The three boys and I, using the bars in front of our seats, unconsciously pushed the bus up and tried to hold it back all the way down. When we pulled into Cimarron, Colorado, not too late that afternoon, we were all exhausted. Or at least Joe and I were. We checked into the small motel there, ate supper, and Joe and I went in to take a nap.

While we slept, the three boys decided to explore the mountains, something we had not anticipated. When we woke there wasn't a boy in sight. Calling got no response.

The people at the motel, used to ignorant flatlanders who didn't know the dangers of the country and its creatures, sounded their klaxon, and at last the sons reappeared. We didn't know whether to kiss them or to kill them.

The next day we moved through Montrose and down into the desert of Utah, heading toward Green River. It was hot as Hades (no air conditioning inside, and the road was as hot as a griddle). We pulled out to stretch our legs, only to find that the right rear dual tire was melting like bubblegum.

"It's just going to have to rain," Joe said. We were still a long way from anyplace, and at about forty miles an hour it takes forever to cover ground. It got hotter and hotter—and then it clouded over and began to rain. With occasional ice in it. We drove into Green River, Utah, to find people standing out in the downpour, staring upward in disbelief. At that time (1968), they told us, it had been five years since they'd had appreciable rain. There were good-sized children who had never in their lives seen rain.

We checked into a motel that gave a wonderful view of the buttes that loom over the town. After eating supper, we went to bed, but Joe couldn't seem to settle down. He had the feeling that something was going to happen. At about midnight, a drunk came fumbling at our door, to be met by my large and determined husband, automatic in hand. Needless to say he made no problem, and Joe slept like an infant for the rest of the night.

There were no tires to fit the bus in Green River, so we headed out toward Price and Salt Lake City. But it was Sunday, and nothing was open that had suitable tires. We limped through Salt Lake City, more and more concerned, and came at last to Tremonton, Utah, where there was a huge truck stop with every size tire imaginable.

There was also one of the most welcome and charming small motels I can remember. Deep, old-fashioned beds, handmade doilies—it was wonderful. And, next morning, we went on our way northward, over the old highway that wound along the course of the Snake River, going through every small town, up and down the irregular terrain flanking the river. It was a most interesting route, now destroyed by the straight, flat, highly efficient interstate highway. We collected large numbers of frustrated drivers behind us on the upgrades, but always we turned out to let them pass, when there was a chance.

The green valley of the Snake seemed like the "green pastures" of the psalm, and for the first time I had a real understanding of much of the imagery in the Bible. We who live in well-watered country have no way to comprehend in full the metaphors of a desert people, which come to life unmistakably when you pass through arid country.

There were signs along the way—humorous ones like IDAHO WATERMELONS painted onto water-rounded rocks that studded the countryside. Today's self-conscious highway bureaucrats would probably cringe at the thought, but such things made what could seem like a deadly journey into fun.

Late that afternoon we crossed the Snake into Oregon. Ontario provided a motel, from which we set off the next morning to cross the "easy" last leg of our journey. This involved "pushing" the bus over seven passes. They've now been cut down considerably, but then they were steep, and the bus was heavily loaded, and we were just about tired out. By the time we came down the descent into Central Oregon, we were anxious to see the end of our journey.

The ponderosa pine forest came as a welcome relief. While Santiam Pass was a stiff pull, the lakes along the route, the huge fir trees, and the fresh scent of the air told us that we had made no mistake in setting our goal.

Already I was looking for a place to stop, to dig in roots and make a home again, but we were still some distance from Corvallis, our initial goal, and only small sawmill towns lay along our route. Near one there was a log cabin for rent that I still regret not checking out.

We came at last to our destination, almost ten days after setting out. It was registration time at the university there, and there was nothing for rent anywhere.

We searched out the countryside, finding at last an old house between Independence and Monmouth. It lay amid mint fields, a relic of what I call Swedish Victorian architecture.

It was a way station, cheaper than a motel, from which we could find a solid rental house. I liked its looks, but once we had camped there we found oddities. While lying in bed, I could see out through the front wall. The front closet smelled strongly of cat, a scent we could never eradicate.

It began to rain. Straight from a Texas summer, we found it so cold in the high-ceiled house that we either took steaming hot baths or went out in the van with the heater on in order to get warm. Our youngest son became ill, and that was when I realized there were "things" wrong with the house.

To give James medicine in the night, I crossed the large living room, which was connected with the kitchen by a wide arch. At the back corner of the kitchen was a doorway leading up a narrow stair to an upstairs room, which we did not need to use.

I have never been afraid of anything, but when I crossed that cold, dark space I could feel that door as if it were imprinted in ice on my side and face. The feeling was incredibly chilling, depressing, and might have been frightening to someone with good sense. I still get goose-pimples when I think about it.

When son Bill explored that upstairs room, he found a trapdoor, beneath which lay a mummified cat, secured within a space not much larger than a boot box. Once he was removed, we thought the smell might decrease. It didn't.

And what was the secret of that house? Though we moved out in a couple of weeks when we found a nice rent house in Silverton, Joe traveled through Independence and Monmouth on the automotive supply route he established in the next couple of years. While serving his route, he heard the story at last.

The people who had lived there had an odd reputation. They seem, according to rumor, to have had highly unusual leanings. When they moved away, they left their dogs locked into a shed, where neighbors head them crying and found them. They left their cats locked in that front closet, to die of hunger and thirst, in desperation and agony. People who would do that would do anything. I don't even want to guess what they did in that upstairs room.

* * * * * * *

In Silverton we came to rest, first renting for a year and then buying an old farmhouse outside town, where we lived for the next six years. It was there I wrote my first two novels. In Oregon we found friends, work we liked, and country we enjoyed exploring for seven years.

We came home again, of course, leaving behind a lot of friends, good memories, and a part of our lives. We used to go back frequently, for I wrote books using my Oregon observations for backgrounds.

I have always wanted to write a novel about the Oregon Trail, particularly since taking, in our own peculiar way, our own way west in the tracks of the emigrants. I feel, in an odd way, that I, too, have been an emigrant like those of whom I write. I know the smell of the desert by day and by night, in sun and in rain.

I can understand the joy they must have felt when first seeing the green valley of the Snake, and their relief when their journey was at last coming to an end. I have been there, and perhaps that has allowed me to give some hint of their feelings and reactions as I followed them along the Oregon Trail.[9]

---

[9] This first appeared as the Author's Note at the end of *High Mountain Winter*, published in 1996 by Berkley Books.

XIII.

DON'T THREATEN A TEXAN

1970

Once we settled into a house, Joe went about finding a way to make a living. He tried several things before taking over running a service station in Silverton, where his mechanical skills served him well. The station was on a corner. Across the side street was a church, and behind the station was a line of small and shabby cottages that backed onto Silver Creek.

This is important, because in those lived a family that had intimidated the town for years. The brothers (three, if I remember correctly) peddled drugs and their sisters with equal energy. Very soon one of them approached Joe with the proposition that he let them use the station for their drug operation. Joe told them, with true Texas emphasis, that if they sold drugs where he could see it, he would turn them in. If they tried selling them to our boys he would kill them.

Let me mention here that we found, in seven years there, that all too many Oregonians are wimps who will not resist intimidation. These bad hats were Oregonian to the bone and unused to such straight talk. They took their problem to the man who was, we believed, behind their operation. A lady who worked in his store took regular trips to Texas (the coast, where we felt sure she picked up drug shipments), and she knew about our kind. "He means it," she told them.

They thought about this for a while. They offered Joe free use of one of the sisters, and he laughed at them. Then they brought in some "muscle" from Portland, forty miles away, brought him to the station, and tried to finagle Joe off his premises so they could beat him up. Instead he came home that night and asked me where my handgun was.

I asked, of course, why, and he explained the situation to me. Those idiots had mentioned, in the hearing of the employee who kept the station while Joe came home to supper, that there was "all that money" going home with Joe every night.

Joe had talked with the local police about the drug selling, and those idiots (or participants?) stationed a marked police car across the street for a couple of days. He told them that if they would not handle the situation, we would. They grinned sheepishly and said, "Just be careful."

We dug out the automatic. Then I got out the 30.06 deer rifle. The next evening I drove to town and parked in the church parking lot diagonally across from the house in which the villains lived. Across the dash lay the rifle, loaded but without a cartridge in the chamber. As I watched the house, I saw that the youngest brother was standing at the screen door, gazing back toward the station where Joe would soon be coming to his parking space.

I took down the rifle and jacked a cartridge into the chamber. This gun is a 1903 Springfield, and the action sounds like a steel trap snapping. When that snapped, the boy jerked like a puppet on a string and turned to stare at me. As I worked in Salem every day and was almost never at the station, they knew nothing about me. Now they were faced with an unknown with a gun.

I sat there for quite a while, as the brothers came to the door, stared at me, then disappeared again. After a time, people began coming out of the house and piling into their (small) car. Three brothers, two sisters, several children, and the muscle from Portland came out one by one and piled into that car like clowns at a circus. Wide-eyed, they drove along the street, turned into the parking lot, and came around some distance in front of my car, where they stopped to size me up.

When they started to move I readied the rifle, letting the barrel trail casually out of the window. As they stopped, staring hard at me, I stared back, looking as mean as I could manage to, with the gun obviously ready for action. As was I. If those lowlifes had threatened my husband, I'd have shot the entire bunch and taken whatever the idiots who run the law in Oregon could throw at me.

Evidently that came through, for they gunned their engine and got out of there, and for the rest of the week that I "rode shotgun" I never saw hide nor hair of them again. Silvertonians warned Joe that they would burn our house, kill our cattle, all sorts of dire forms of vengeance. What they actually DID was to cut the water hose at the station one night. We never had any trouble with them, though months later their car came up our steep and winding road and ran into the ditch. Joe thought perhaps they all got hopped up on their own drugs and came out to try to "get" us, but were too stoned to drive straight.

XIV.

GOING HOME AGAIN

1975

Every time we moved out of East Texas I got sick. My roots seem to be so deep in this soil that when they are pulled up I wither on the vine. That was true when we moved to Houston in 1964—we spent eighteen months having flu, chicken pox, etc.

When we moved to Oregon, the climate was so benign, the land so gorgeous, and the town where we settled so pleasant that I thought we'd stay there forever. Then it was back to respiratory problems and increasing problems anatomically—I will not be too specific. Just say that I was a Jersey on one side and a Holstein on the other. The doctors couldn't make it be cancer and wouldn't admit any other possibility, and things got worse and worse. (When I got back to our family doctor in Texas he diagnosed it at once—I had mastitis! A course of antibiotic cured it right up.)

About that time the gas shortage of 1973 happened. Joe had a service station and it was a hassle getting gasoline. The Oregon economy went to pot. We took a while deciding, but by 1975 we'd determined to come back to Texas. We both knew we'd be broke when we returned, though selling our house and two acres outside Silverton provided a bit of elbow-room.

We rented a big U-Haul truck this time. Joe drove it, with his van attached, and I drove my Plymouth Sundance behind, as we took off for home again. In August of 1975 we were back and looking for a place to rent or buy, its only specification being that it had to be in the country. We found one, a small and flimsy frame house with ten acres, which we eventually bought. We camped in that house for seven years, the last two of which we spent building my present home.

This is a strange structure made of diamond-shaped twenty-gauge aluminum panels, connected with almost 3,000 nuts and bolts. Its design makes it resistant to wind damage and impervious to burning debris from a forest fire. It looks something like a spaceship and contains generations of family antiques.

Including me, of course.[10]

---

[10]Our time in Oregon and the trip home again were utilized pretty thoroughly in my mystery novel, *Deadly Memoir*.

XV.

A FOWL STORY

As children we often make rash vows: "I'll NEVER do this, that, or the other." Usually we have our noses rubbed in every item on the list. I was no different. Over the years I worked that list down to one, "I'll NEVER raise chickens."

So we moved back to Texas, and with the place we bought we acquired two broiler houses capable of holding more than twenty thousand broiler chickens. For two years I tended those brainless wonders, and in that time I could breathe through my nose only between batches of chicks.

That was mean work, beginning with the delivery of the baby chicks, which huddled beneath the big gas heater hoods, trampling each other to death, or drowned in their own water trays. Every morning and every afternoon, they had to be fed and watered and the dead picked up. It was a relief when they were old enough to go on the automatic feed and water systems.

Broiler chicks are de-beaked to keep them from eating each other (theoretically—I found they did it anyway).

One rainy winter morning, clad in slicker jacket and hat, boots, and gloves, I was filling the feed bin. This involved a power switch on the wall that turned on the auger that brought the feed in from the huge tank outside, filling the big bin from which the food went out along a track. I had to smooth the feed in the bin to keep it from spilling over the edge, and on this morning I left it a bit late and had to dash across the track to get to the switch.

I hung my toe and fell flat on my chest, knocking the wind out of myself. As I lay there trying to regain my breath those little devils were trying to eat me alive, their beaks sounding like hail on my slicker and hat. Only the slicker, boots, and gloves kept them from doing it, and even then the gap between my gloves and sleeves was pecked into hamburger.

Chickens attract all kinds of nasty predators. Skunks will go through a house full just killing chicks and sucking out their blood. We had a war with those until Joe poisoned their den.

Chicken snakes were a constant problem (remember that I hated snakes). I found a pair, once, with half-grown chickens halfway down their gullets. That gave me time to go to the house and get the .22 so I could kill them.

While tending the chickens for the weeks required was a pain, cleaning out the houses was worse. This was done with a shovel, throwing the manure into the pickup to be hauled off. I wrote some very good poetry while shoveling manure, both on the dairy and on the broiler farm. My head seemed to get as far as possible from what my hands were doing.

Anyway, I have done penance for the last thing on my list of things never to do. I take care not to say, EVER, anything more positive than, "If I can help it, I'll try not to do that."

That's the safest way.

XVI.

BOOKSTORE AND REBELLION

Joe tried several different businesses after we returned to Texas. He took over a service station, again using his mechanical skills to augment the income, and that worked fine for a number of years. However, the gas consignee who leased the station to him died, and his successor was determined to make ALL the money, while Joe did all the work. Once more Joe was looking for a job. He went to work at a local Firestone store as shop foreman. When they told him he must support their lies when they told someone they needed repairs that were unnecessary, he quit. The day he came home after quitting that job, I got a huge (for me) royalty check.

With that sum we prepared to open another bookstore, a used book shop this time. We had enough duplicates in our personal library to form a pretty good stock. We also made a trip to Oregon on a bit of the money, and while there we visited church bazaars and garage sales and picked up a load of books that were different from those marketed in East Texas.

For several years I had written a weekly column for our local newspaper that I called VIEW FROM ORBIT. That seemed like a good name for a bookstore, and it had name recognition. So View from Orbit opened its doors in September of 1984, and we went into our second incarnation as bookstore operators.

This gave us a unique insight into the local government, as our customers were extremely bright individuals, some of them lawyers, some county employees, most of them interested in the long-standing corruption of Nacogdoches County politics. Our shop was a hotbed of good talk on every subject imaginable, but more and more often that talk centered on the county government, which was at that point exceptionally bad.

We organized a Concerned Citizens group. When members called state offices to inquire about methods of reform, more than one was told, "When the subject of local corruption comes up in Austin, Nacogdoches County is the first name that comes to mind." Reform it? They would just laugh.

Principally with the help of several brilliant and determined women, this group managed to accomplish more than one difficult and sometimes dangerous task. Threats through the mail and via telephone and harassment of several petty kinds ensued, culminating in the destruction by fire of the home of our president and the deaths of her two sons in that conflagration.

There was no serious local investigation of that, and when we contacted the FBI (there had been threats through the mail, remember), the agent sent to talk with Joe and me lied through his teeth. Only afterward did I learn that to be true, on discussing the situation with a fellow writer who had been a CIA agent. The local deputies questioned her neighbors, thus: "Don't you think she set that fire herself?" There was never any finding issued in that case.

I never much trusted the government, having observed entirely too much lying over the years. Now if officials deny something vigorously or insist upon something energetically, I assume either is a lie. It usually is.

In 1992 Joe was diagnosed with a pancoast tumor in his spine. Even then, we continued to write letters, appear on radio programs, and to support opponents of local incumbents. Not until 1998, when he became really ill (not the cancer—radiation had taken care of that—but with respiratory problems) did I have to turn loose of the political situation and concentrate on taking care of him, running the bookstore, and doing all the necessary work around the house.

In September of 1999 he died. My sons helped me dispose of the shops (by then we had a computer shop as well), and they moved everything usable to create an office at home. There I could continue instructing for the Writer's Digest School, do my own writing, and augment my independent book doctoring business.

I had faced the loss of Joe in 1992 when his doctors told us his chances of surviving his cancer were very small. I lived with that facing me for seven years. When it actually happened I was exhausted, and had already done my grieving....

...I thought. I never had the chance to find out, for on October 17th, the very next month, I was driving to Chireno after my mail when I swerved to miss something on the wet road and had a wreck. This totaled my little Sundance, compressed my T-5 vertebra by 50%, shattered my left ankle and foot, and proved to me that I, too, am subject to the laws of physics.

After orthopedic surgery, I was in the hospital for about a week. My dear sister took me home with her, where different therapists visited me to get me mobile again. By Christmas I was at home again, my son Frank having come for Thanksgiving and stayed with me until the new year began. By that time I was pretty well mobile and could drive, which made all the difference.

I now live alone and thoroughly enjoy it. I cannot see the house of any neighbor in any direction. Once you get past my road you are getting closer to someplace else, which is why we picked this location. It's about as far from civilization as you can get, bar moving into the Big Thicket. So I have returned to being a loner, and am glad to be at this point.

XVII.

INTERVIEWS

OCTOBER 1995

Q: Talk about where you grew up, went to school, where your roots are.

A: My mother's family migrated into East Texas before 1830, and my roots are so solidly planted here that every time I have ever moved away I have become ill. Though I was born at my grandmother's house in Timpson (Shelby County), I grew up in Nacogdoches, forty miles to the southwest.

    I graduated from Nacogdoches High School in 1947, a fractal-cornered character amid a bunch of well-rounded ones. The education we got there rivaled that of many college graduates today. In addition to a solid grounding in the basics, math, and science, I studied Spanish and Latin, paving the way for my fascination with languages. For ten years, I ran my father's dairy and studied French, Spanish,

Italian, Latin, German, classical Greek, and delved into Egyptian hieroglyphics, history, and the sciences. I never went to college (except to teach).

Q: What career or other jobs did you have before you started to write? Or was writing something you started to do very early?

A: My dad and I used to swap rhyming lines at the supper table, when I was two. We created sagas about grasshoppers, buzzards, and crawfish. I was a poet before I could write. I wrote poetry (dozens of published poems and a chapbook) until I was forty-three and discovered what I was going to grow up to be, which was a novelist. I wrote my first science fiction novel when my family lived in Oregon. I worked as a proofreader at *The Capital Journal*, made a huge garden, kept a big house, and had two children in school. Every Monday afternoon I wrote a chapter of my first and second novels, and in a year I had finished both, which were also my first published books, *The Seekers of Shar-Nuhn* and *How the Gods Wove in Kyrannon*. Along with writing, I have been a dairyman, a proofreader, a grower of broiler chickens, a bookstore owner/operator, a political activist, lecturer, and instructor for Writer's Digest School. I've been married for thirty-eight years and have two stepsons, two own sons, two grandsons, via the stepsons.

Q: Talk about how you started to write. Did you start with articles, short stories, true crimes?

A: As I mentioned, I began as a poet and have continued to write and publish poetry. My first novels were sf-fantasy, but I soon wandered afield into young adult fantasy, westerns, horror, and historical novels dealing with pre-Columbian Indian cultures. Science fiction and fantasy are great fun, but once you get far enough from your roots and look back, a wide perspective opens up. At that point, I began writing about things I know intimately or have learned through prior interests. My East Texas stories are, I believe, among my best, and my book *Slewfoot Sally and the Flying Mule*, from a small press, is a collection of family tales, folklore, and tall tales from this area that have been gleaned over my entire lifetime.

Q: What was the first material you sold and to whom?

A: I sold my first novel to Doubleday on its second trip out to market. The editor who bought it left, and Pat LoBrutto took over, buying five or six more from me during his tenure there. This first was *How the Gods Wove in Kyrannon*, which is linked by its context in an invented world, though not otherwise, to *The Seekers of Shar-Nuhn*, *Warlock's Gift*, and *Lords of the Triple Moons*, a young adult novel published by Atheneum.

Over the years I have hiccupped short stories, too, and have had work in *Twilight Zone*, *Isaac Asimov's Science Fiction Magazine*, *The Magazine of Fantasy & Science Fiction*, *Marion Zimmer Bradley's Fantasy Magazine*, *Fantasy Book*, several literary magazines, many anthologies of suspense/mystery stories, fantasy stories (three of Andre Norton's *Cat Fantastic* books), and a number of small press publications.

My first published western, *Feud at Sweetwater Creek*, came from Zebra under the byline Frank Cannon. They swore the public bought a third fewer copies of westerns under female bylines. As much of my mail comes addressed to Mr. Ardath Mayhar, that made little sense to me. Zebra published two more, *Bloody Texas Trail* and *Texas Gunsmoke*.

My first book for children was a collaboration with my childhood friend, Marylois Dunn, whose first juvenile novel was the prize-winning *The Man in the Box*. *The Absolutely Perfect Horse* came from Harper in 1983. That hooked me on writing for children (I never got over ten years old myself), and I followed it up with *Medicine Walk* (now a Houghton Mifflin choice for its reading series, BEYOND THE REEF) and *Carrots and Miggle*, both originally published by Atheneum.

Over the years I have written quite a lot of books on contract, beginning with one of the FASA BattleTech novels, *The Sword and the Dagger*. For Byron Preiss's MILLENNIUM novels for young adults I created a First Contact novel, *A Place of Silver Silence*. Several years ago, a packager signed me to create the Mountain Majesty books, written as John Killdeer. I wrote the first six of them for Bantam, relinquishing the task to another when my health became undependable. Amid all this, my agent sold to Berkley my first pre-Columbian Indian book, *People of the Mesa*, which concerned the cliff dwellers on Mesa Verde. It was followed by *Island in the Lake*, *Towers of the Earth*, and, in 1995, *Hunters of the Plains*.

Q: Talk about your current books or series of books.

A: I have completed my work on the mountain man series, and interest in the Indian books seems to have waned. At the moment I am free as a bird and am writing a number of short stories that crop up like boils.

Q: What books are to be released near term? What projects do you have in work? Talk about the direction of your writing:

A: In March, 1996, Berkley will publish as part of its Jove line *High Mountain Winter*, a story of the Oregon Trail, under the byline Frances Hurst (for marketing reasons that would make a goat laugh). At present I am writing on three novels, *Small Bird*, a book for young people about a child left orphaned and reared by Crow Indians; *Lone Runner*, a book about a young woman sold to a terrible master, who flees down the Snake River; and *Born Rebel*, using my own family background in the early part of the nineteenth century. My researches into history have given me a wealth of material, and there are several more Indian books that I would love to write, if we can find a market for them.

I also would like to push my small press books, which include *Through a Stone Wall* (scheduled for October publication), which is a collection of articles, talks, and workshops I have published and/or presented at writers' conferences and in my work as an instructor of fiction writing. In fact, it is my belief that midlist writers are going to have to move in the direction of the small presses or into computerized distribution, as the multinational corporations that now run publishing have just about ruined the market for original and unusual work.

I also will continue in the WOMEN WRITING THE WEST field, which has just become a recognized sub-genre. And I will continue being a MEAN LITTLE OLD LADY!

Q: What are your favorite characters in your books?

A: Asking about my favorite characters in my books is like asking me which is my favorite child—the answer is ALL OF THEM. Still, Uhtatse, in *People of the Mesa*, is one of my favorites. He still lives inside me someplace. My Soul-Singer, from *Soul-Singer of Tyrnos*, is another. I began that book by seeing her dusty boots swinging forward in the road and feeling her compulsion to fulfill her work, and she has never altogether left me, either.

Carrots and Miggle may be my favorite book, because it reflects the strange child I was and it also shows the dairy I ran for many years. The plot may be fictional, but that dairy and that odd little girl are real. *Medicine Walk*, too, is close to my heart, for I lived that story with Burr Henderson, heard the cougar growl, and felt the awful need to lie down and die and the dreadful compulsion to rise and go on, as he did. But it is *People of the Mesa*, a story about the Anasazi on Mesa Verde, that I consider my best work so far. It required four years to write, dropping chapters on my head like bricks when it got good and ready. I did little rewrite, once I had all the parts assembled.

NOVEMBER 1995
(FOR FIONNULA WILLIAMS)

I write just about everything except romance. My western stories have been set in the past, so far (Mountain Man era, the Oregon Trail, pre-Columbian Indians), though *Medicine Walk*, my children's book, is a contemporary story. That book is now part of Houghton Mifflin's middle school reading program, Beyond the Reef.

I have traveled extensively in Wyoming, Colorado, and Montana. While researching my novel *High Mountain Winter* (due from Berkley, March, 1996, under the Frances Hurst byline), I retraced the trail itself, following it all the way through South Pass and beyond. *Lone Runner*, a novel in progress, begins in the area east of the Bighorn Mountains (about 1863) and moves cross-country to the Tetons and beyond into Idaho and the Snake River Canyon.

I began writing as soon as I could hold a pencil, after creating long poetic epics with my father since about the age of two. I wrote poetry, placing much of it, until I was forty-three, when I realized I was, at heart, a novelist. Since then, I have completed fifty-seven books, all but one of them novels. My mother read to me from the beginning (that is a good way to hook a child into reading). Jules Verne probably roused my interest in science fiction, and Joseph A. Altsheler almost certainly hooked me on historical novels set in the west.

The day I got my first acceptance for a novel, I was alone on our country road (everybody worked in town, except me—I was raising broiler chickens) with no one to tell. I told my dog, the mockingbird in the redbud tree, and almost telephoned my mother, though she had been dead for several years at that time. By the time my husband came home I was about to BURST. That was in 1977, and the book was *How the Gods Wove in Kyrannon* (Doubleday, 1979), my first sf novel.

My favorite of all my novels? That's like asking which is my favorite child. But I still recall *Soul-Singer of Tyrnos* (Atheneum, 1980) with particular affection. The pictures that formed in my head as I wrote were incredibly colorful and gorgeous. I lived the story with my protagonist, and I wish the book were still in print. I enjoy all the genres, but I seem to have "fits" of westerns, of science fiction, fantasy, horror, and mystery. Sometimes I have books in all the above going at the same time.

XVIII.

LETTERS

July 18, 1995

Dearest Evelyn,

    The problem with the bio stuff is the fact that it doesn't interest me. I already know everything about it. What makes writing fiction fun is that you create it from scratch, which is fascinating. I am putting down many of the things I remember, principally for the children and (if ever) grandchildren. They will have a record of things they took part in, with details they may not remember, and they will have a glimpse of what went before. This particular piece was written as the afterword for *High Mountain Winter*, my Oregon Trail novel, so it couldn't be long or involved, anyway. You get the detailed stuff in the novel.

Love,

Ardath

August 15, 1995

Dearest Ev,

    We did have a most successful trip, in every possible way. We got home late Wednesday night, the 9th of this month, and we both feel better than we have in a long time. Simply getting out of this climate for a while seems to have helped a lot.

    We had a lovely, if short, visit with Bill and his family. Then we took off down the coast highway, all the way to Big Sur, where Jackie's Dad was waiting for us at the camp ground in his camper pickup. A friend of Frank and Jackie was also there, having arranged to meet us all—he was a lovely person, French from Canada. He is a science fiction fan and likes my work, and we had a lot to talk about.

    Frank and the family arrived about two o'clock in the morning on Saturday, having been stalled when the highway was closed because of a big forest fire. Three hours in a traffic jam in hundred degree heat is no fun. They and Elena camped in tents down in the camp spot with the two men, and Joe and I had a cabin right across from the bathhouse.

    The campground is on a little river and set amid huge redwoods. It is a family place, so peaceful that you can relax completely. The people who run it are charming, and I gave them a couple of books before we left. It was completely full all three nights we were there.

    Jackie and I went to Carmel on Saturday, for we needed groceries and we also wanted to look into some art galleries, which we did. Talking all the way, I might add, for we have MUCH in common. On the way back we pulled into a viewpoint and got out. The fattest spotted squirrel you ever saw or dreamed of came right up to my feet, stood on his hind legs, and demanded FOOD! No excuses accepted!

Jackie tore an end off the loaf of sourdough bread she'd bought for her Dad, I broke it in two, and the squirrel and his slightly smaller (not much) mate accepted it grudgingly as only their due. We laughed all the way back. Those squirrels are prime candidates for strokes or heart attacks, if you go by their obesity.

Frank had to work Monday, so they left late Sunday afternoon, after sitting around the campground talking a blue streak. We stayed until early Monday morning, when we headed out eastward. We spent the first night in Kingman, Arizona, and the second in Santa Rosa, N.M., getting home about ten-thirty the third night.

Along the way I got ideas for several short stories, two of which I have already written and sent off to market. I have the terrain needed for one of the books I'm working on, as well.

Of course, there was a pile of lessons waiting for me to correct, but I am working my way through them slowly and without being impatient (much!). I'd better get done with them—I have three different lecture/appearances to do in September.

Love,

Ardath

To Katharine Eliska Kimbriel, 1996

Dear Kathi,

    Actually I am having fun with a small press publisher near Houston. She's a remote cousin of mine, actually, and we are on the same wavelength. She has done two books for me (in addition to some other books of poetry, etc., under her imprint).
    Slewfoot Sally and the Flying Mule has done well so far. We do very small printings (she has her own equipment), so we can meet demands that come later, when there has been a chance for word-of-mouth to build up sales. We sell to mailing list customers, and we are getting ready to hit bookstores, when we get our Universal Marketing Code number. *Through a Stone Wall* is my book on writing. We have had only a tiny printing so far, because her father became ill and died, and she has only just gotten back on the job. We are pushing it to creative writing teachers in high schools and colleges.
    She uses my own art for covers, and future editions of *Slewfoot* will have small drawings at the ends of chapters. She does a lovely job of printing (photocopying, but she has one of those terrific copiers), and the books look fully professional.
    I also collected a bunch of my published poetry and created, using my own drawings, a book, which I had printed in California before my cousin and I joined forces. I find this hands-on method most satisfying.
    Otherwise, I keep getting older and crankier. Long trips are getting beyond me, though I intend to keep going to AggieCon as long as my son James is working on his

doctorate down there. By the way, you made a HUGE impression on the cadre of Mayhar men who visited with you a couple of years ago. Three sons and a grandson, if I recall correctly. They all raved about you.

Love,

Ardath

April 27, 1996

Dear Yawl (as my Dad used to begin all-purpose letters to friends and family):

I hate these, but so much has happened and so many of you need to know about it that this is the only way to get you all informed. I still owe Marj and Mona and Kathi and Alice and Jayne Ann letters, but this will have to do for now.

Early on Monday morning, almost two weeks ago, Joe awoke with a sudden and terrible pain in his upper right chest wall under his arm. It was so bad he couldn't walk to the van, and I had to call 911 and have the ambulance come out after him. He was taken to the Nacogdoches Medical Center and stabilized (it took almost two days to get his temp and blood pressure up and his white count down a bit).

They checked everything—gall bladder, heart, liver, the works, and could find nothing wrong until they did a CAT Scan, which showed a mass between his right kidney and his pancreas. He was kept on ice chips only for a long time + I.V. all the while he was there. As the local doctors felt exploratory surgery might be indicated, we transported him to Houston to the VA Hospital where all his other "miracles" have taken place.

He arrived in Houston on Friday (22nd? I think it was) and for most of another week he had either no food or liquids, because they were taking scans and biopsies and felt the need to be prepared to do surgery, if an emergency should arise. For ten days he had no food, only ice chips, then liquids, and only the last two days of his stay did he get a real diet.

Biopsies showed only blood in the mass, though they found nothing internal that was bleeding. The mass had encapsulated and may have been there for quite long time. I finally thought to ask him, on Thursday the 26th, if his pain was his usual "old" pain he has been controlling for four years or if it was the new one that sent him to the hosp. They had kept him on Demerol, so he wasn't able to make the connection until I asked. All his recent pain had been the old familiar array from the first cancer four years ago.

Joe was unwilling to undergo exploratory surgery, and once his doctors realized that the initial pain had disappeared under the onslaught of the high-powered antibiotics given at both hospitals, they allowed him to come home (yesterday). It is my opinion that the violent pain was the result of a virulent infection that yielded to antibiotics. The mass may well have been discovered simply because they were looking for a reason for the attack. Whatever it is, it is only blood, and evidently they found no cancer cells in it.

Frank, his fiancée Dayna, and her daughter Jordyn flew from California, and I stayed with them at a wonderful hotel, Harvey Suites, where we had a kitchen so we could eat there. They also supply shuttle service free to the hospitals and also to points of interest and restaurants. Because of that Frank didn't have to rent a car, and we didn't have to eat out. Although the suite was not cheap, when you count the saving on a car and on restaurant meals for a week, the cost was more than reasonable. Besides which, the people driving the shuttles and at the hotel were remarkably helpful and courteous.

Bob (oldest son) and his fiancée came from Jasper on Saturday, and James drove over from Bryan, where he was in the middle of his final examinations for his Ph.D. when I called him about his Dad. James spent the night with us in the suite, though Bob and Rebecca had to return Saturday night. (James passed all his finals. Has the orals April 30.) When Joe had his first cancer in 1992, James was in the middle of finals for his Bachelor's Degree. I hope he doesn't go for any further degrees—there seems to be something dangerous about that.

I had been having a terrible problem with my (long abused) back. Evidently the rush of adrenalin (plus the work of my chiropractor) cleared up the problem instantly, and I had no trouble during the two weeks it took to get Joe back on his feet (at least, comparatively on his feet—he's still weak and wobbly). Now that we're back home the back is tightening up again—may see the chiro this week.

Two weeks before Joe became ill, I got a royalty check from HarperCollins for $9,000 (sub-rights to Simon and Schuster's educational line). This was not for a book but for a short story, one of ten or so in an anthology for girls. I felt the company must have sent me everyone's sub-rights money for some mistaken reason, so I called to tell them I thought they had sent me too much money. I have a call from the company that came in while I was gone. I do hope I don't have to send it back, but I expect I will, some of it. At least it was comforting to have it in my account during all this *sturm und drang*. (Must repay half, as I suspected.)

The store was manned by one or another of four volunteers among our friends/customers, almost all the while we were gone. Nobody has customers like ours, believe me! They accept no money, be it known, though I intend to give them something, if only books, to show our appreciation.

We intend to go in to work Monday, though I expect Joe will have to lie down on the cot in the back room for part of the time. I have twenty or so corr. school students' work waiting for me, plus one of my independent clients. Cross your fingers that I catch up—then I'll write individual letters to all of you.

Fantastically,

Ardath

To Alice Lindenborg, 2001

Dear Alice,

It is so good to hear from you—I had wondered and wondered when I got no reply from the last letter.

I can't recall how long it has been, but in case it has been two years I'll recap briefly. Joe died Sept. 7, 1999 of chronic respiratory distress. There was no cancer in his system! I had already moved the stuff I wanted from the shop, and the boys helped me close out the last of that responsibility. I now have an office at home with computers (four), copier, FAX, printers, etc. Of course, except for my school work I am doing very little writing. You know how losing a loved one shuts off your valves for a long time. Things are beginning to move again, now, but slowly.

In October of 1999 I had a car wreck that shattered my left ankle (plate and screws hold it together, now) and compressed a vertebra. I was in the hospital for over a week; then my sister took me home with her until I could fend for myself. By Christmas I was living by myself at home and doing pretty well, considering the wheelchair and all. By this spring I was getting around well without even a cane, most of the time (but you knew how tough I am, didn't you?).

October a year ago (2000) I was invited to the Beaumont Writers Conference and there an agent I have known for years asked if she could represent me. I was amazed, shocked, and pleased. We met again later that month in Corpus Christi at World Fantasy Convention, where she made a deal for selling reprint rights to two out-of-print books to Stealth Press, a new publisher specializing in hardback reprints. She is also marketing a lot of my unpublished work.

The sons are all well. James got his Ph.D. in poly-sci last August and now has a good job near Dallas, where his wife is an executive with Verizon. Frank just married a lovely Chinese lady, and I hope this time it works for him. He married two very needy women before, and his own clinical depression didn't help things a bit. Bob, the oldest, remarried and lives not too far away. He is a postmaster.

All in all, things are going well. I am not doing much, being just about worn out. I have put my white charger out to pasture and others have to do the crusading now. Do stay in touch!

Affectionately,

Ardath

To Karen Rankin, February 16, 2001

Dear Karen,

I am glad I am on propane here. I can control that much more easily than I could natural gas, which went up 60% this year.

The staph seems to be cleared up (used Lotrisone cream, after the yeast infection due to the Levaquin, to finish the job). I am having terrible allergies, however, along with everyone I know. The weather has been dreadful, and elm trees are blooming full out, which seems to have filled the air with pollen.

I can't seem to get my writing enthusiasm going. I have two short stories started but can't seem to keep moving with them. I am tired, I think, and the weather is such that I can't get enough exercise. It is lucky that my agent has so much material to work with—I may or may not ever complete another novel.

There is a lattice at the front of the house with vines growing up it. A possum—and family, I think—has been climbing onto the house, which is curved like a Quonset hut but with deep indentations to let water run off. I think they are playing soccer up there at night, using either an acorn or a hickory nut as a ball. You never heard such a clatter in your life, and then someone loses his balance and goes scra-a-a-ping down the slope, trying to dig in with claws. Makes for interesting listening after I go to bed.

Do enjoy your new home and let me hear from you when you have the time.

Affectionately,

Ardath

July 24, 2001

Dear Karen,

Moving is one of the most traumatic things in life. I can still remember where things (books, mainly) were in the old house, sixteen years ago, but where they are now is a total mystery. So I understand your dilemma very well.

It has now begun to get HOT. We had a very mild summer through June and most of July, but last week it got up in the high 90s and low 100s. I have air conditioners in the front and back of the house, and I use one at a time, moving the air with ceiling and box fans. Electricity here went up a lot this year, though not, thank heaven, as much as I am sure yours did out there.

I finished one of those stories, but the other is still hanging in mid-air. I am working on a new one now, and it is going well. For the first time in a long while I find myself really wondering what happens next. I hope this is a good sign.

The humid heat makes my knees swell and my bad ankle hurt like crazy. My chiropractor tells me that is because the metal, the skin, and the bone all expand and contract at different rates. This means that I can't take long walks, though when it is cool enough I do take very short ones.

Oh, and now the cats have begun to practice for the summer Olympics on my roof. This morning I woke to terrific thumps and thuds—sounded like wrestlers slamming each other onto the metal. At least three must have been involved, for a single cat couldn't possibly thump in three spots at the same time—or could he?

I started a book a few weeks ago. Just taking it as it comes, without trying to push. Maybe it will be completed and maybe it won't, but I am not worrying about it. I do have some really great scenes so far.

Things go pretty well for me, actually, though I am shutting down my life neatly as the opportunity arises, to save the boys trouble when the time comes. They are all settled and as happy as people tend to get, which makes me very happy.

Besides, I now understand the old statement, "I'd move to Hell from Texas." My thermostat is not what it used to be!

Stay well

To Andre Norton, October 17, 2001

Dear Andre,

Two years ago today I had the wreck. Strange feeling, learning that the laws of physics apply to me, too! And here I am walking fine, getting around about as well as I would have if nothing had happened at all. One thing about being an East Texas farmer—I am tough.

Stealth Press has taken its time over the contracts for *Hickory Hollow* and *People of the Mesa*. Cherry W. has been pushing them, but you know how impossible that is with publishers. No movement on any of the other books she has in hand that I know of—I still think nobody wants my stuff any longer.

I'm down to six cats now. The big tomcat has run off both young ones, and one of my mama cats got run over. Her daughters, luckily, finished raising her kittens. With the coyotes in the pastures and the alligator in the creek, outdoor cats live a dangerous life.

There is an obstreperous squirrel living in my red oaks at the front of the house. He uses the WORST language you ever heard, when he catches a cat looking at him or finds a snake up in his tree. And at night he bombs the top of the house with acorns, I think. It sounds like a war up there.

Living in the country is interesting, believe me. I can't see my nearest neighbor's house, which makes it nice and quiet. As you will see from my return address, I have discontinued my post office box (it was a ten-mile round trip to get the mail), and now get it in my route box free. This helps some, as living on Social Security is a real adventure.

I write a short story from time to time, but I have not yet conjured up enough energy to work on a book. Maybe that ability is gone for good.... I had a pretty hard knock on the head in the accident, and sometimes that can change your thinking.

You are truly amazing, the way you are staying busy.

Take care of yourself and have a nice Halloween and Thanksgiving.

Fantastically,

Ardath

To Arlene Krenz, August 6, 2001

Dear Arlene,

I hate to hear that you are having more heart problems. Those are no fun—my Dad had heart trouble for twenty-two years. At least you will now have family across the road to help you with things, which should be a comfort.

So far, this has been a weird year. Cool and wet through June, not a drop of rain in July, hot as the toenails of hell so far this month, but then yesterday we had a good solid rain—about an inch. It is cooler today, which is a great relief.

Evidently we chose our home site well. We are above flooding levels, on a ridge. That is between two higher ridges that usually carry tornados high over our location. When I hear a train in the middle of the night I know there's a twister way up there, on its way to someplace else, because the nearest railroad is twenty miles away. Thus, as yet, neither wind nor flood has affected the house.

I am well, though the weather has had me feeling pretty miserable, as 100 degrees with 90% humidity keeps my knees and legs swollen and my energy level low. If I survive August (and February), I usually feel that I have it made for the year.

School work has dwindled a lot, and I have quit writing for the time being. My agent is handling the many books I had on hand when the market changed, as well as the dozens that are now available for reprint, so there is no great pressure to create more. That is good, for when it is this hot I really need to do nothing at all. My blood pressure reacts badly to intense heat.

The book sorting I mentioned earlier is going along well. I have sent fifteen big boxes of sf to my friend in Michigan, and as I go I find other books I really want to re-read. My book cases are still full, just not triple-stacked, and now they hold volumes I am re-reading. This helps me pass the long hot days.

Living totally alone as I do, there are weeks when I see nobody, unless I happen to meet someone at the post office. If I were writing it would be ideal, but there is still no energy to work on new material. I am not letting it bother me, though, which is one good thing about getting to the age of seventy-one (I got there in February).

Take care of yourself,

Ardath

Feb. 1, 2002

Dear Arlene,

    I will be seventy-two this month. Feels strange! Inside I am still ten years old!

    We had very warm weather for a couple of weeks, ending yesterday, when we had hard rain and a cold front come through. Today it is raw and damp. Even with the heat turned high it is hard to get the house warm enough. Luckily I use propane, and my big tank is still half full.

    I am so glad I no longer have to lift five gallon cans of oil to fill the old oil heater. The old body got so it was having trouble with that, shortly before Joe died, and he insisted on getting the propane tank and heater. Thank goodness!

    My best friend since childhood has been in the hospital with pneumonia, then in rehab. It has kept me busy taking her things she needs from her house, and when she gets out I hope to bring her out here with me for several days until she is steady on her feet. We've been friends for sixty years.

Business has been good since Christmas. I have been getting more lessons from Writer's Digest School and have also had a couple of large book doctoring jobs. This is a great relief, for I was very strapped for money much of last year. I hope this will continue through the current year. If I can make it for another seven months, my van will be paid for and I can live on Social Security, if business slows down.

We have had goldfinches coming through already, very early for their migration. This indicates an early spring, but I would have guessed a hard winter and we haven't had that yet. The spring peepers were croaking earlier this week, but the cold spell has shut them down.

Stay well and warm!

Ardath

March 30, 2002

Dear Karen,

Let me answer your questions first: I live twenty-five miles from the nearest town of any size and five from the nearest grocery store. There is contracted local garbage pickup, though mine is picked up by a black friend my husband used to help. There is no recycling to speak of, even in Nacogdoches where our store was. They simply don't think it's important enough to bother with. If I had enough recyclables to count, which I don't, I could take them to Lufkin, thirty miles away.

I am on a septic tank, one of the big round cement ones. Those seem to be the most durable and trouble-free. This has been in service since 1984 and has never given a bit of trouble, as I add Rid-X every month.

Last weekend I was at Texas A&M at AggieCon. This was the thirty-third annual sf convention there, and I began going in 1980. I have missed only two or three along the way, so I see a lot of really neat people once a year. The student center where it is held is big and floored with terrazzo, and I walked entirely too far and climbed too many stairs. My foot and ankle have given me billy-heck since I got home. I may not go again, as the drive makes my crushed vertebra hurt like blazes.

I do miss my piano—I still have my grandmother's, which was made in 1902, but it needs re-felting and tuning. I can't afford to have this done, as re-felting would cost something like a thousand bucks. As it is, you strike a key and the hammer hits the strings and sticks. My mother was a piano teacher, so I learned very young and always enjoyed playing just for myself. If I am ever able, I may buy an electronic keyboard.

You know, many creative people tend to be fragmented. I love to paint, to embroider, to make music, to write poetry and prose, to work with flowers...just POTS of things! I always called it having "fits of painting" or writing or whatever. Just followed along where my instincts took me and then changed when the time came.

Fantastically,

Ardath

December 4, 2002

Dear Arlene,

You are wise to get ahead with your Christmas greetings. I have mine in progress, just a few a day. If I do too many at once my back gives me fits.

We had a lovely Thanksgiving. James, my youngest, and his wife were here on Wednesday and Thursday, and we had such a nice visit. I don't know certainly what we will do at Christmas, but we always manage to have a nice one.

I am giving my family copies of my unpublished books for Christmas. I can't afford to buy stuff, and they really don't need anything, for they buy what they need as they go along. This will be something that can't be bought anywhere. I have a heavy duty stapler and staple the books together, with the end pages protected by plastic sleeves. They are easy to handle and to read.

It has been raining like mad here for two days, inches and inches, some of it very hard downpour. The temperature has not been terribly low, but the forties seem very chilly when it is raining. I suspect the creek bottoms are flooded, but I don't intend to go and see.

A couple of my favorite people are coming this holiday season. My foster daughter from California will be here the fourteenth, and a "borrowed" son, also from California, will be here in early January. That will be a lot of fun. As long as I don't have to travel, I love seeing people. Riding for an hour or more gives my old back FITS, so I don't do much of that, any more.

I hope you have a great Christmas. Stay well and keep in touch.

Love,

Ardath

To Dr. Annette Carney, *Novelists' Ink*, 2003

Dear Dr. Carney:

After reading your column in *Novelists' Ink*, I venture to hope you may have some advice for me. In 1992 I had sold some thirty novels, and my husband and I operated a bookstore/computer shop. In April of that year Joe was diagnosed with a pancoast tumor of the spine. Radiation reduced the cancer, but over the next three years he was treated for two more cancers. When he wasn't in the hospital he was at work, but I had to keep the businesses going, my novels meeting deadlines, and basic needs taken care of.

Following seven years of increasing illness and frequent hospitalizations, in 1999 Joe died (chronic respiratory distress). The next month I had an almost fatal car wreck, which compressed a vertebra and shattered an ankle. I survived and have healed (I'm now seventy-three), but I cannot think of beginning a new writing project without getting a cold, sick feeling in the pit of my stomach.

I wrote sixty novels and dozens of short stories in the space of twenty years, and not writing makes me feel very empty. Except for occasional short stories, I seem unable to begin anything new, though I am able to lengthen or shorten existing unpublished novels.

Is this a part of the grieving process, the healing process, or simply burnout, do you think? I am tough, live on Social Security and what I can make teaching for the Writer's Digest School, and do what is necessary as to housework, but if I cannot write I feel extremely useless. Being the world's most incurable optimist, I am not depressed, but if you have any advice that might help me "turn on my writing switch," I would appreciate your letting me know.

Thank you,

Ardath Mayhar

Feb. 7, 2003

Dear Arlene,

Thank you for the lovely card and notes. My youngest son James and his wife want to come soon and walk over my ten acres and her father's fifty acres, looking for shuttle debris. By now you know that debris from the *Columbia* was scattered all over Nacogdoches County, in downtown Nac., and in Chireno. They had to close the school, for a piece fell through the roof. I was standing at my front door checking the temperature when the rumbling began. I thought we were having an earthquake, for the house shook, the ground shook, and the TREES shook.

As the thing pounded overhead, I kept hearing explosions, which were probably impacts from things falling in the woods. Later that morning there was a sharp chemical stench in the air, probably hydrazine and some of the other nasties from the propellants.

Saturday night, shortly before ten o'clock, I heard an army truck (nothing else sounds like those) growl down the county road in front of my house, sounding as if it were followed by several other vehicles. I suspect they were either following up on a sighting of debris down toward the river or checking for that.

Most of the human remains were found at Hemphill, some twenty miles from me as the crow flies. I cannot imagine what it must have felt like, finding parts of people on the ground after such a disaster.

As far as I know, nothing landed on my ten acres, but that is overgrown with brush and grass, and I have not been able to walk over it since my accident, which is why my son wants to check it out. I can't struggle through the overgrowth, and if I could, I'd never make it back up the hill to the house.

Anyway, I came out fine. My sister put it best: "Anything that took you away would have to come from a lot farther off than a space shuttle."

Take care of yourself and continue getting better.

Love,

Ardath

May 16, 2003

Dear Arlene,

It sounds as if you had a really wonderful Mother's Day. We used to love to travel up toward Hood River and along the Columbia Gorge. Gorgeous country!

I had calls from all my children on Sunday. That made my day, for going places is no longer something I like to do, since my crushed vertebra gives me fits because of the motion. My traveling days are over, and I don't regret that, for Joe and I got all that out of our systems during his last years.

You won't believe this—I have sold my last-written fantasy novel! A small but professional press in Staten Island, NY, is preparing the contract right now. Not a lot of money, but some, and they intend to ADVERTISE it. Wow! *Riddles and Dreams* is the title, and there is another book, if they decide they want it, that is a sequel.

I had begun to think nobody wanted my stuff any more, and this has made me feel a lot better. A mystery is also out to another small press. Cross your fingers.

I am staying busy and feeling pretty well, and I hope you are the same. Take care of yourself.

Fantastically,

Ardath

December 9, 2003

(Reply to letters from students who read *Medicine Walk* in school)

Dear Students,

As many of you want to know the same things, I am going to write this letter something like a story, with everything in order. I will be seventy-four years old on Feb. 20, 2004. I was born in Timpson, Texas, at my grandmother's home, though my parents lived in Nacogdoches, about which you may have read in Texas history. I spent the best parts of my young life on my grandfather's farm near Timpson, where I roamed the woods with my younger brother, fished in the ponds, and enjoyed camping in a log cabin, using a wood cook stove and going down a woods path to a privy, with owls hooting in the trees overhead.

After my grandparents died, my own parents bought a farm near Nacogdoches, where we went into the dairy business. I helped to build the dairy barn and, after graduating from high school at the top of my class, I ran the dairy for the next ten years, following my father's near-fatal heart attack. Because of the need for my services, I did not attend college, but I did continue to study.

In those ten years I studied poetry, literature, Latin, Greek, Italian, French, Spanish, and German, ancient history, the theory of mathematics, painting in oil and watercolor, and music. As you might guess, as soon as I learned to read in the first grade I was off and running, reading everything I could get my hands on, and our house was full of books.

After running the dairy until I was twenty-seven, I bought my first bookstore in Nacogdoches. There I met my husband, who worked just round the corner while going to business college. We married in 1958. My husband had been married before and had two sons, Robert (now fifty-three) and William (now fifty-one). We then had two sons, Frank, who is now forty-three, and James, who is now forty-one. Robert is postmaster at Kirbyville, Texas, William is retired and lives in Oregon, Frank is a software engineer in California, and James is a statistician working for the Burlington Northern/Santa Fe Railroad.

In 1968 my husband and I moved with our sons to Oregon, where we lived for seven years. On the journeys to and from Oregon I developed an interest in the mountains and the plains country, as well as the Indians who lived there. Still, when I wrote my first book in 1973 it was a fantasy, as were the next several ones.

I began writing poetry as soon as I could hold a pencil, and continued to do that for many years. After moving to Oregon, ideas for books began to pop up and HAD to be written. Nobody really inspired me to write, but my father and grandfather were wonderful storytellers. Listening to their fascinating stories of their childhood, I just absorbed storytelling into my bones.

My first two books (on the enclosed list) were written in Oregon. We moved back to Texas in 1975 and I continued to have story ideas struggling with each other as to which would be written next. Over the next several years I wrote many more, encouraged by the sale of the first book to Doubleday in 1978. Every one of these is still exciting to me, for as I wrote I saw the story inside my mind as if I were watching a movie. All I had to do was write down what I saw.

When Ace Books asked me to write *Golden Dream: A Fuzzy Odyssey*, it was a great honor and a wonderful experience. It was the royalty from that book that allowed my husband Joe and me to start our second bookstore in 1984. We ran that until 1999, when Joe died.

Although I never made BIG MONEY, the added income was very helpful, particularly when my husband became ill with cancer n 1992. Along with the bookstore, that income allowed us to live comfortably and to make trips back to Oregon, where my stepson Bill still lives. In 1981, on such a trip, we checked into a small motel in New Mexico. I was sitting on the bed, making notes for the book I was researching on that trip, when the picture of this small plane (a Cessna like one in which I learned to fly, many years ago) and its occupants appeared. As I watched, the father clutched his chest, the plane went into a dive, and the beginning of *Medicine Walk* happened before my eyes. I have written another novel about Burr Henderson, but editors changed at my publishing house and the second one has never sold, though I think it may be even better than the first.

Several of you asked if I am an Apache or know Apaches. No, I am not and have not, but I have spent many years in researching American Indians of various tribes, the Apache among them. I do have an adopted grandson who is a Halifa Indian, however, a daughter-in-law who is half Indian and half Irish, a granddaughter-in-law who is Hispanic, and a daughter-in-law who is Chinese.

Over the years I have: 1. Run a dairy farm, 2. been a professional proof reader, 3. operated a bookstore (twice), 4. been an instructor in writing and a "book doctor" for unpublished authors. I find that nothing you do is ever wasted, if you are a writer. Good things and bad ones all go into your storytelling and make it seem real to the reader. It is not easy to write a book, and nowadays it is even harder to get one published, but writing is something you can't help doing, if that is what you were born to do.

Some of you asked about my free time. Being elderly and somewhat disabled, I have a lot of that now. I still work for Writer's Digest School as an instructor in short fiction and novels, as well as doing critique work (something like grading papers, actually). I do editing for new writers. I keep my short stories going out to magazines. But in between I read and read and read. My favorite sort of book is a good mystery, but I read a lot of other things: history and science and philosophy. I, too, love the Harry Potter books. I also like the movies made from those, as well as *The Lord of the Rings* movies. *Stargate SG-1* is my favorite TV show.

Some asked what other job I would like, if I were not a writer. I would have loved to be a ballet dancer, but I was born with trick knees. That pretty well washed out that option. I also paint, from time to time, in watercolor. I've sold some of those, but art is a very difficult profession in which to make a living.

You may wonder why I use more than one name on my books. It is usually the publisher who decides that for reasons of marketing. Zebra decided that a woman's name on a western means it sells fewer copies, so I took my great-grandfather's name, Frank Cannon. Berkley invented the John Killdeer line for the Mountain Man novels. For *High Mountain Winter* I used my middle and maiden names, at their insistence.

Of all my books, I probably like *People of the Mesa* best. This one took me four years to complete, and it came to me as Joe and I drove down the mountain from Mesa Verde, where the cave dwellers lived. Entire scenes just dropped into my lap. This is still available from www.fictionworks.com in electronic format.

I no longer write new stuff, though I have a lot of completed books that I am marketing. I think my accident did something to "shut off my faucet." A new book, *Riddles and Dreams*, is available from:

www.imagespublishing.net

I now live alone in the middle of the East Texas woods in a house that looks like a space ship. Two outdoor cats keep me company. A squirrel and his family live in the big red oaks in front of my house. A possum sometimes visits my deck to see if the cats have missed some scrap of food, and a raccoon has been known to peep into my front screen door to see what I am doing. Though Joe and I used to raise cows and calves, when he got sick it was too much work and we sold them, so our ten acres has grown up into brush and trees.

I never cared for team sports, preferring things like fishing and reading for hobbies. I still read constantly and take as long walks as my injured ankle can manage. Because I don't quite like to risk going down to the Attoyac River (a few miles down my county road) alone because of my unsteady walking, I no longer fish.

I hope those of you who said they wanted to write will relax, enjoy living, and take notes of interesting things that happen, so you can use them later in life. Ideas come from good and productive living and I wish you all that sort of life, with plenty of ideas and time to put them onto paper. By the way, the computer has made writing MUCH easier than it was when writing by hand.

Sincerely,

Ardath Mayhar

November 24, 2002

Dear Karen,

Something rather strange and wonderful happened last week. I have always believed that the mind can heal the body (and itself) if given the chance, but that is hard to manage. Last Monday night I had a dream: On a large grassy plain stood a red stone shaped like Ayres Rock in Australia, though it was only table-sized. Around it were children, using the top as a drawing table. They had placed big sheets of parchment there and were drawing pictures of skeletons.

I pushed aside the drawings and laid my hands flat on the warm stone, which tingled like electricity. The tingle went all the way through my body, making me feel as if I might levitate. When I woke the next morning I felt wonderful, even having some energy. My bones didn't hurt and though they have begun to ache again it isn't nearly as painful as it was before. Inside, I feel different, more positive and able than I have for years. Besides, the dream is adding an entire new dimension to a story I have been working on!

Are you familiar with 1-800-homeopathy (www.1800homeopathy.com)? A friend ordered me their #006 Cough/Hoarseness tablets, and my allergies shut off like magic. As for Vitamin E and gingko—I have taken both for years. One reason I survived the wreck so well, I think, is because I have taken supplements/herbs/etc. for so long. I have gone backwards through glasses until I am now three prescriptions into the past. Bilberry had done a fantastic job with my eyes.

Being almost seventy-three and feeling as if I am getting younger is rather spooky, isn't it? Take care of yourself

Fantastically,

Ardath

April 17, 2003

Dear Arlene,

What a lovely Easter card! Thank you for thinking of me. The weather here is wonderful at this time of year, warm by day, still cool to chilly at night. The trees are fully leafed out, most of the spring flowers have finished blooming, and roses are coming out wonderfully.

Before Joe died he bought what was advertised as a Paul Scarlet Climber rose. It bloomed for the first time last year, and it is not that, but a gorgeous very deep red—almost black—rose that opens very slowly and has a wonderful shape. I have had one open in a bud vase in the house, and another cluster is on its way on the vine.

I also have an antique Chinese pink rose that looks like a huge bouquet just outside my living room windows. Dutch irises are beginning to bloom fully, and my red amaryllis buds will open before long. This time of year is my favorite here. Later it will get very hot.

Cross your fingers! I may have a sale for my only remaining unpublished fantasy novel. Images SI in New York State has asked to see the book, after several phone conversations. I would love to get this one out, for so many people have asked me for another fantasy. Two mystery novels are off for consideration, one to Pocket Books and one to Hilliard and Harris.

Since January I seem to have a bit of energy—enough to manage to write queries to smaller publishers whom agents have not approached with my work. In a couple of days I may whomp up enough to wash my van, which looks awful after a winter standing beneath the red oaks in the front yard.

I have seen a red-headed woodpecker in my front yard, along with many cardinals, thrushes, finches, towhees, chickadees, catbirds, and mockingbirds. The orchard orioles are back, though they are so small you can't see them. Only by their songs can you know they are here.

I hate to hear that Richard is having such trouble with his driving. When Joe got so he couldn't drive I took over, but I don't know if you learned to drive. I don't know what I'd do, being twenty-five miles from town, if I couldn't drive.

Take care of yourself,

Ardath

To A. R. Morlan, July 26, 2003

Dear A.R.,

I was thinking about you yesterday, wondering how things are going with you. As for me, several rib-heads came out of their sockets along my spine recently, in the middle of the night. I think I must wrestle gorillas in my sleep. The worst mishaps of late years have happened while I was fast asleep.

My chiropractor is snapping me back together, but it has been very painful, and I can't manage to work for more than a half hour at a time. As there is a lot of critiquing to do, this is a bother, but I am managing.

You sent a nice batch of clippings this time. I am particularly interested in the Indian ones, the thirteen women who were tested as astronauts, and the one about Nefertiti's bones being found. There is some great material there.

It is hard getting work done, particularly when there was so much damage in your area. I have had a few things needing attention, but luckily a friend has recommended some great plumber/electrician/carpenter types who have done excellent work for me.

Marj sent me an e-mail last week telling me that *Writer's Digest* is publishing a special supplement listing dependable proofreaders and book doctors. I have sent in my specifications and hope they will put me into that, for the extra work would be helpful.

Do take care of yourself, and thank you for everything, including the refill of stamps. You spoil me!

Affectionately,

Ardath

Dec 18, 2003

Dear A.R.,

I am hoping to go Saturday to the movies and see *Lord of the Rings*. Having bought the videotapes of the first two, I have watched them again to catch myself up and get in the mood. I can hardly wait!

A couple of months ago I had a phone call from a former student, who has moved from Alaska to Virginia. She is such a neat lady, and she volunteered to send me a crystal from Vermont, specially charged with "new energies" that are supposed to have healing powers. Strangely enough, since I received it and put it beside my chair, I have felt better and better and even have had extra energy.

I didn't actually believe it would happen, and not until I began wondering why I was feeling so well did I put it together. So either it was simply time for me to heal or the crystal had some effect. However, as long as it worked, what does it matter?

Thank you so much for the stamps. I keep sending things out and getting them back. Sadly, I just learned that Vincent Kuklewski, editor of *The Black Lily*, died recently. He had accepted several of my historical stories and paid me for one of them. I suspect the magazine will fold now, which is too bad.

I hope you have a wonderful Christmas and that you both are well for the entire season.

Affectionately,

Ardath

Jan. 26, 2004

Dear Karen,

Sad to say, the Writer's Digest School will be discontinued in June of this year, along with the Critique Service. Their on-line writers' service seems to have siphoned off most of the interested students. This will remove almost half my income, but at this point I have JUST paid off the last of the computer shop debt, so I can live on the Social Security, if needed.

Of course I always have a few private clients for my book doctoring, which fills in a lot of gaps. I will be building up that side of my business, and if you know anyone needing such service, I would appreciate your passing along my e- or mail address.

I will probably put an ad in the *Writer's Digest*, which I felt would be unethical as long as I was doing that work for them. Living alone, I have to have something to do, aside from earning the income. Luckily, I get a lot of phone calls from family, friends, former students, colleagues who live at a distance, even clients who live overseas, and letters from interesting people like you. This keeps life interesting.

Strangely enough, at this point I am feeling better than I have in years. Having a new challenge to face and a new and different project to push forward is stimulating to me. I seem to be a believer in Tao—whatever is happening is the best thing that can happen, if you react to it properly.

The best thing of all is that everything I own is paid for! My current bills and occasional book purchases I take from my ongoing income, and they are minimal. I find myself both comfortable and happy, which is a lovely state!

Affectionately,

Ardath

Jan. 18, 2004

Dear Arlene,

Sorry to take so long to respond to your letter. I have had more company this past month than in the two years preceding it. Fun, but time-consuming!

I have now had time to go over your verses, and I still find myself charmed by your work. I found only a couple of small corrections to make, but I am returning them to you. I know how difficult it can be to hand copy or get to a place to photocopy work like this. I do urge you to make books of these for your children—they should be delighted to get them.

I am sending with this a postcard I bought years ago at a showing of the local art league. I thought you might like the scene, which is VERY East Texas. Our country roads do have bridges like this, some of which wash out in big rains or collapse under log trucks.

I am again a preliminary judge for the self-published book competition of the *Writer's Digest*. This is a lot of fun, for I get forty books to read and assess. In the past two years, almost all of those have been excellent reads, only a handful being poorly written. I find a lot of less-than-professionally-written novels on store shelves, believe me.

My new book came out in October, but there has not been time to know how well it is selling as yet. I hope it does well, for this small company is wonderful to work with, and may, if this does well, publish the sequel to it.

For the first time in several years I have a bit of energy and feel quite well. I hope it lasts! There is even a bit of appetite now, which has never been the case with me in my life.

The cats are thriving. My black one that decided to become a tomcat has run off the mean visiting tomcat, so Max, the other visiting tom, has returned. He is a sweetie. When my stepson and his bunch were here before Christmas, his little grandson was playing out in the front yard, wanting Max to ride in my little wagon. Of course Max objected, though he was polite about it.

We were looking out, watching them, as Tonio sat on the deck, shook his finger in Max's face, and said, "Young man, look at me when I talk to you!" I thought his daddy was going to fall out of his chair he laughed so hard.

I hope you are as well and happy as I am. Have a wonderful new year!

Affectionately,

Ardath

April 13, 2004

Dear Karen,

I wish I could "magic" to you the vision in my head when I wrote the scene in *Exile on Vlahil* in which the vlammalba and the vlammere waltz in the air. That was the most gorgeous thing I ever saw, in or out of my imagination.

Things continue to look up for me. Since I wrote I have received a letter from Bruce Coville saying that *The Unicorn Treasury*, in which I have a story, is being recontracted for a mass market edition, with a larger advance than I got the first time around.

Then Joe Lansdale urged me to query Golden Gryphon Press, asking if they would like to see *Two-Moons and the Black Tower*. This book was contracted by Doubleday and the advance was paid, but almost immediately the company was sold (that big acquisition in which so many of the publishing "fish" got devoured by the whale). My agent died, my editor left, and though the book was listed in their catalog, it was never published. Anyway, I queried, and the editor at G.G. has asked to see synopsis and sample chapters. Cross your fingers!

Some time ago I re-read Ursula Le Guin's *The Language of the Night* (a collection of essays and talks on writing fantasy), which gave me a psychological boost of major proportions. I wrote her a letter of appreciation, and we have begun a lovely e-mail correspondence. She has agreed to recommend my book doctor services to would-be writers who approach her wanting such help. She no longer finds it enjoyable to do such work. Funny thing, we are both seventy-four-years old. 1930 must have been a vintage year—she and I and Marion Zimmer Bradley all were born then. She, too, has been having problems with creative energy. This may be more an age thing than anything else.

I got about six pages into the chameleon story and it dried up. Maybe it will come back to life, given time. Sometimes I go back to story leads I wrote years ago and am able to complete them. By the way, your suggestion about my old Indian in *The Adapter* is interesting. I'll play with the notion and see what happens. I have been having a serious case of the "don'ts" for the past few days.

I do agree with your comment on tastes (mostly abysmal) and values (mostly contemptible) in today's culture. As to our current administration, if we do not make a drastic change, our entire way of life is going down the spout. Have you noticed that there is almost nothing beautiful being done in drama or movies or art or music? Even "serious" composers are creating cacophony, for the most part.

I'll look for the "Party of One" book. Sounds interesting. Have a good time on your getaway.

Fantastically,

Ardath

March 12, 2004

Dear Arlene,

After a very LONG WET winter with more cold nights in a row than I can remember in recent years, it has finally warmed up. Although I had been feeling very well before, I now feel even better, and have been watching the trees begin to bud and the spring flowers start doing their thing. In fact, I felt so good that I: 1. vacuumed the living room, 2. washed the van, 3. cleaned the oven, 4. wiped down the front windows as far as I could reach.

When you consider that it had been months (maybe even years) since some of those got done, that is pretty amazing.

I was glad to hear that they are maintaining Silver Creek Falls State Park. We used to go up there quite often, when we lived in Silverton, and the last trip we made to Oregon, Joe and I went up there and walked as far as he could hold out, filming videotape all the way. That's a lovely place.

My cats are singing love songs, so there will be kittens before long. I hope my mama cat raises this batch—she usually disappears when they are due, reappears in a few days, and I never see hide nor hair of kittens. I'm the only person I know who has a perennial shortage of cats.

After a very long while, I am presently working on a short story. I have no idea if I will be able to finish it, but it feels good to be working again, other than my teaching and critiquing. The Writer's Digest School is being discontinued as of the end of June, so I will need clients for my book doctor work. If I can get back to doing my own work, as well, that will be a great help.

Take care of yourself and stay well.

Love,

Ardath

May 15, 2004

Dear Arlene,

For several weeks I was wrestling with bronchitis, which I have now subdued. Not coughing all night is a wonderful luxury!

I got well just in time to go to my oldest son's home in Jasper sixty miles away, to speak to their local writers' group. This is a pretty large organization, and even though this whole area was under a tornado warning almost all day, there were some thirty people present for my talk. There were all sorts of writers, from poetry to historical nonfiction, and all ages were present, even a little girl about eleven years old, who wrote poetry.

Much to my surprise, an old friend from Beaumont (which is about another sixty miles south of Jasper) was there, and we were able to exchange e-mail addresses. They seemed to find my talk useful, and of course it was funny, for writers must laugh at the business or else we'd do nothing but scream and moan.

The drive down was hellacious. Driving rain, highways awash with water falling too fast to run off, and, of course, that ever-present warning of tornados. I finally stopped at about 2:45, after hearing on the radio that Jasper County was under a severe tornado warning until three. I found a Dairy Queen and had a milk shake while I waited until three. By that time the rain had slacked off to a simple downpour, and the rest of the journey was easier.

I had calls from all the boys and some of my "borrowed" children on Mother's Day, but I didn't do anything much personally. That suited me fine. Bob's home is at the end of my "leash," for I can travel for an hour, no more. Then that crushed vertebra begins to hurt worse and worse and worse.

It has rained for almost a week, as front after front goes over us. It is thundering right now, and there is a good chance of more rain today. I am tempted to go down to the old house and dig out the aluminum fishing boat that is overgrown with weeds and vines. Though I am on a ridge, if things go on, I may need it to escape from my island.

Cross your fingers for me. I have a proposal out to Golden Gryphon Press, and I would love for them to publish this book. Doubleday contracted for it just before the company was sold, and the new owners never published it.

Do stay well and keep busy. That is my prescription for a good old age.

Affectionately,

Ardath

July 13, 2004

Dear Arlene,

There is good news on the home front. In the first week in June an editor called who was ready, many years ago, to buy two stories from me when the magazine died on the vine. She now owns her own e-publishing/trade paperback company, which is specializing in getting back into print the work of authors of past years. She wants not only my out-of-print work, she also wants to publish the rest. The juveniles, the short stories, the many novels that have not been published are on her want list.

Thanks to e-mail, we have already signed a contract and I have sent her (via attachment) a number of books that were on disk. She also will scan into her system the books written pre-computer, and she offered even to scan manuscript.

Although I had been having certain health problems, this has made me feel ten years younger. Indeed, I have lost the symptoms I was having and am feeling better than I have in a long while. After so many years of being rejected by so many publishers, this is a most gratifying development.

I hope your hand and arm problems get better quickly. Being unable to write can be a pain, all by itself.

Take care of yourself and stay well.

Love,

Ardath

August 4, 2004

Dear Arlene,

I LOVE the pansies! I may save this and stick it up someplace to cheer up gray days. The photos from Detroit Lake are great, as well. I may send them to my sons, who have wonderful memories of their time in Oregon.

I hope your new well is up and running by now. Having lived on a well almost all my life, I understand the problem. Just before Joe died, he arranged for the municipal water supply to be extended to our place. It was expensive, but it has kept me from having to deal with pumps going out, etc. The water is not loaded with iron, as was our well, and that helps too.

Your computer and you did a great job with the letter. This speeds things up a great deal, as well as saving wear and tear on the fingers. I have now great need of my computer to access the internet, but my main Int. computer has had its modem die, and my backup computer can access the Internet but cannot write to or access its disk drives. AAAARGH! as Charlie Brown used to say.

I am going to have to buy a new system, I am almost certain. I thought I could go along using my two systems, but when this happened I thought, Somebody was trying to tell me it's time to get a new outfit. My editor sends the material to proofread as a Word attachment, and I copy it to disk and correct it, then return it as a new attachment. Can't do that without a system that works together.

She is doing not only the books and short story collections, but also my poetry and maybe even some of my newspaper columns. Everything will be on her system, ready to go into electronic versions and then into trade paperbacks at the rate of one every two weeks for several years to come.

As you can imagine, I am most pleased about this. If your daughter wants to pull up the site, go to http://renebooks.com, click on the link at the left, and there will be *The Crystal Skull and other Terror Tales*, so you can see what the site looks like.

Stay well and busy!

Affectionately,

Ardath

August 20, 2004

Dear Arlene,

    A series of storms keeps coming through every few days, and instead of being steamy hot, August (so far) has been unusually cool. Yesterday a front came through, and I think a small tornado—or at least a pretty strong whirlwind—came through my front yard, picked up a lot of bamboo I had trimmed, and spun it around for several minutes. I got 3½" of rain, too.

    A week ago a tornado came right over me, luckily above treetop height, dipped and destroyed dozens of trees north of my place. It broke off or uprooted BIG oaks and pines. The road crews are still clearing up and/or cutting down trees that threaten to fall over the roads. I feel as if the tornados are doing "ranging shots" to get my bearings, so if I disappear into the wind just think of me exploring Oz.

    I am glad you had such a nice visit with your sister. Getting together with family is always fun. I am lucky to have my own sister nearby (within forty miles), and my oldest and youngest sons relatively close.

    I do plan to buy another computer system. We have decided that an IMac will be best, as those are immune to most Internet viruses. James, my youngest, found that they can read both WORD and text files, and I can buy an external disk drive for this, so as to use my existing diskettes. Luckily, my book doctoring business is thriving, so I can easily afford this system.

    I had hoped to finish out my life using my old systems, but one is twelve years old and the other is seven years old. Both have begun giving me occasional problems, and my book doctor business requires both Internet access and a reliable computer. The new publisher sends my upcoming work (like galley proofs, only via e-mail), so I must use it for that as well. I'll let you know how this works out.

Do stay well and cool. I feel fine unless I get too hot, at which point my blood pressure goes way up. I am not having to use my air conditioning very much this summer, as it has been so cool, but I have learned not to allow myself to get too hot.

I am glad Richard gave up on the baling. Must be a relief to you.

Affectionately, Ardath

August 30, 2004

Dear Arlene,

No, I don't do storm cellars. Being a life-long claustrophobe, I'd rather be "Gone with the Wind" than cramped underground. Probably with water moccasins for company. It doesn't flood here unless we get a foot or so of rain, and even when it does, my place is on a ridge. Our snakes are mostly water snakes, so they have no problem with rain.

Actually, I looked out of the window at that little tornado, and the next day I found it had pruned the dead branches out of my oak trees and carried the debris totally away. Also swept off the dead leaves. I'd just as soon have more traditional gardeners, however.

The photos are lovely. I might try doing a watercolor of one or two of them, if you don't mind. I don't get the painting urge often, any more, but maybe the impulse will strike.

I am still very busy—the book doctoring work picks up steadily, which is a great addition to my Social Security. Very helpful!

We used to have a cougar that would come through here every couple of years. His paw print was the size of a plate, and I once found where he had "done his duty" and covered it, just like a cat, but it was the size of a wash tub. I never minded them—there are usually enough rabbits and other small game to take care of the big cats, who tend to be very thin on the ground.

Take care of yourself.

Love,

Ardath

Sept. 30, 2004

Dear Arlene,

My trip to Dallas couldn't possibly have been better. The Lansdales and I talked hard all the way up there, which was fun. Then I was on four panels, plus an "Hour with Ardath Mayhar," moderated by Joe Lansdale. We had great fun, and afterward all the books I took with me sold out.

I had no pain at all, which was surprising. Evidently I have healed enough so that riding is no longer so painful. I had energy to spare, and I was not exhausted when I got home. I am planning to get in touch with the committee at AggieCon next spring to tell them I think I can come. This will be the first time in three years, if I manage to go.

The books are coming up at Renaissance E Books every two weeks. Then they are picked up at www.fictionwise.com. In a couple of years they will begin coming out as trade paperbacks as well. My first mystery novel, *Closely Knit in Scarlatt*, is already up—there are four more to come. At this point Renaissance has forty-three books in their system, five or six of which are available as electronic books.

The day we left for Dallas, the end of Hurricane Ivan came through East Texas on its second trip and flooded a lot of country. Luckily, it never got as far north as Dallas. While I was there, my son James and his wife came and got me and took me to their home, which I had never seen because of the pain of riding. It is a gorgeous place (she is an executive at Verizon, and he is a statistical analyst for Burlington Northern/Santa Fe). We had a lovely visit.

I hope St. Helens settles down and behaves. You certainly don't need a replay of what happened before.

Did the printout of my painting arrive? I thought you might like to see the sort of art work I used to do. This is, of course, a scanned version of the original watercolor, printed out via computer. I have on order a machine that does color copies, acts as a printer and a FAX, and may even wash the dishes. That will make copying my work even easier.

Your trip up the mountains sounds as if it was very satisfactory. I remember how the vine maples used to brighten up the terrain. I understand that it is the action of vegetation that breaks down the lava so it eventually becomes soil. That, by the way, is the richest possible soil, for it contains minerals brought up from the depths of the earth and never leached out by rainfall.

Stay well and busy!

Affectionately,

Ardath

October 8, 2004

Dear Arlene,

I did enjoy the sf convention a great deal. Along with Joe Lansdale, I was a special guest, which meant the con picked up the cost of my hotel room and paid Joe gas money. I felt great, my back did not hurt, and though my bad ankle got very tired, it was not too painful. I sat in on four panel discussions, all of which were well attended and very interesting, and had "An Hour with Ardath Mayhar" all to myself.

This was a fine opportunity to publicize my books that are coming up regularly on the site of Renaissance E Books. I took some printouts of two PR pages my editor e-mailed to me and passed them out. We sold ALL the books I took with me for sale, and of course the Lansdales and I talked all the way up there and back.

Just got my first royalty check from Renaissance. After having my work up (only one or two most of the time) for only three months, my check was for $75.00, which promises well for the future. By now they have several more titles on their site, and Fictionwise.com has a cooperative agreement with Ren., and puts the books up there, as well.

We have had rain and more rain for the last two days. This is the greenest summer and early fall I can remember. Usually the fields are tan by late July, but this year the woods and the meadows are as green as spring.

Funny thing—my impatiens plant that I have wintered over in the house for four years has sat on the deck all summer. Several pots of dirt, without plants in them, sat nearby. In three of them are new impatiens plants, possibly propagated spontaneously from fallen leaves? Interesting.

The cats are well and getting obstreperous. I have had to finagle a catch for my front screen door, for two of them have learned to open it for themselves. They are outdoor cats, and I don't want them inside at all. They have other ideas, of course.

Business goes well, with regular input of work from clients and students. In fact, things are going so well that it almost makes me nervous. My luck is not this good, ordinarily.

Take care of yourself and enjoy the fall colors.

Affectionately,

Ardath

October 23, 2004

Dear Arlene,

Thank you for the pictures. I do enjoy seeing the Oregon places I used to visit with my family—these are such a treat.

I'm glad Diane found the web sites where my books are listed. She did just what she is supposed to do—chose a book and printed it out for reading at her leisure and yours. A new one is supposed to appear every two weeks, if the schedule goes forward as planned. www.fictionwise.com is another where they pop up shortly after appearing on Renaissance E Books. That one has a couple of my children's books that do not appear on the REB site.

I think you may like *Hickory Hollow*. This is the way Joe and I would have handled the aftermath of an atomic war, if we had survived in viable circumstances. Too many books about that concentrate on the political and military aspects. I prefer to look at its effect upon individuals in a specific environment.

Funny thing about my watercolors: many or most of them were painted in hospitals while sitting there with Joe through his many serious illnesses. That's why they are small—a watercolor pad that fits on the knee and a vision that can be completed in a short while are ideal for that. Trying to read when you are worried sick is not a good option, but I found I could paint under almost any circumstances. Many of those paintings I gave to particularly nice doctors and nurses.

I brought in my plants off the deck last week. We had cold weather (at least for here) in September, but since I got them inside it has turned hot again—90s by day and 70s by night. Had to use my AC, in fact, which I hardly had to use at all back in August. I am wondering if we may not have a wild winter, as the weather seems to have turned a corner into some new and unpredictable pattern. I had my propane tank filled back in September, when the price was as low as it would get.

Would you believe that at long last I am compiling a memoir? And into it are going many of my letters to friends, including you, going back for many years. That is a great thing about writing them on computer and saving them to disk. They sat there waiting for me to need them. The neat thing about a letter is that it reflects what is going on in your life at that specific time, which gives them a feeling of immediacy.

My editor at REB has been urging me to do this, and all the way back from Dallas, Joe L. kept nudging me to do it as well. I just regret that I didn't do it in time for my friend Evelyn to see it. She nagged me for decades, but now she's gone and it's too late for her to say, "I told you so!"

Stay well and busy!

Ardath

XIX.

PERSONAL PHILOSOPHY

Funny the things you think of when you get older. I began life thinking about such matters, as far back as I can remember. I believe that we are all integral elements of the universe, which is the embodiment of the creative spirit. We create ourselves as we live and begin to die, and when we do die, we are freed into the greater reality, outside the physical world(s). I am afraid I don't believe anything taught by any of the churches or major religions. Those all create tiny little gods no bigger or wiser than they are, ones they feel they can control.

XX.

WHO CREATES VICTIMS?

    The constant plaint from politically correct elements that women or blacks or any other group has been "victimized" by society or white males or whatever is just about to get my goat. You are only a victim as long as you are willing to put up with the label. That is what revolutions and civic uprisings are all about. If you will put up with oppression, you deserve it.

    (Did you know that in England, burning at the stake was continued well into the late eighteenth century for women only, the offense being "treason"? Treason in this sense was defined as defiance of male authority; this should tell you that women have always defied fathers, husbands, and brothers, to the extent that a need was felt for a fearsome punishment for such an offense.)

    For myself, I come from a family in which most of the women have never been victims, as far back as I can follow the bloodline.

    Why? For one thing, it is my contention that women rear daughters either to be victims or to be competent human beings. My ancestresses seem to have been determined people who shouldered their responsibilities fearlessly, and, when possible, took charge of their lives. Such women do not rear wimps or simpletons, and they do not conform to cultural pressures to do so. A victim has to be trained to accept that fate as a just punishment for failings she has been taught to see in herself.

Consider my great-great-grandmother, Martha Cannon, who lived in South Carolina toward the beginning of the nineteenth century. Her farmer father betrothed her to a well-to-do neighbor. On her wedding day, the young man she favored came to the spring where her family got water, and waited for her sister to come with a bucket.

"I am going to Texas," he told the girl. "Ask Martha to come to the spring and bid me goodbye."

Martha came (I suspect with a parcel of possessions in hand), and instead of bidding David goodbye, she got onto his spare horse and went to Texas with him. This young woman was NOT a helpless victim. Though she died young, she lived and died as her own person, not the pawn of an ambitious father.

Her daughter-in-law, my great-grandmother Cannon, was left alone with her children in East Texas when her husband went off to the Civil War. The country was wild and sparsely inhabited. The family were share-croppers, and most of the children were girls, yet the crop work got done and they survived. When Ravenna Cannon came home from the war, devastated with malaria and sometimes bedridden for months at a time, nobody starved. They produced thirteen children, seven of whom, all girls, survived and lived interesting lives.

There was no money, even for schoolbooks, but my grandmother studied a neighbor's books while they walked long miles to school, her sister holding her elbow to keep her from falling into the ditch.

Her youngest daughter, my grandmother Ellington, rode the meanest black horse in Shelby County, sidesaddle. She shot my grandfather's hog-leg revolver so well that even the lowest local bully never dared to approach her as she drove a buggy all day through deep woods to visit her mother, or went about town nursing sick people whom nobody else would touch.

She also made a huge garden and canned the produce, killed hogs and dressed out their meat, made most of her and my grandfather's clothes, along with those of their two daughters, and found an outlet for her love of beauty in music and handiwork. She lived a fulfilled life, and no one ever had the temerity to suggest that she was a victim of anything at all.

Her daughter, my mother, was afraid of nothing. She was her father's "son," became a music teacher, married my father in the teeth of social opposition, and learned from him how to wire her parents' home, when electricity became available in their town. She drove the thirty miles of mud road from Nacogdoches to Timpson to visit her people during the week, when my Dad traveled as a salesman. When her car (this was the Twenties, remember) broke down, she crawled under it and fixed what was wrong. One of my earliest memories is of my mother sitting on the living room floor with the vacuum cleaner around her in many parts, repairing something that had gone wrong. She put it together again, and it worked.

My father made thirty-five dollars a week during the depression. My mother saved half of that in government bonds. When they were ready, just before WWII, they bought a farm and built a house, and we moved into it early in 1942. My brother, my sister, and I were integral parts of the family business, and we all worked together in the fields, milked cows, built fence, all the vital parts of keeping a farm going.

My sister and I would tackle a bear and give it the first two bites (probably even now, as old ladies). We know how to function as fully competent adults, for no other option was ever presented to us. We understand that because we were reared to do it, and the lack of that attitude is one of the terrible injustices that the feminist movement is imposing upon young women today.

Nobody ever had to be a victim, unless she might have been physically or mentally impaired. The victims were trained for that by mothers whose own mothers had trained them to be victims.

The vocal feminists who yell exploitation or victimization are continuing that nasty process. I, as a woman, have done just about everything I decided to do in my lifetime, from learning to fly a little Aeronca with a motor no larger than that of a washing machine to becoming a published author, and I never asked anyone for permission to do it. I never asked anyone for help either. It is not the function of government to make life easy for anyone, rich or poor, male or female, black, white, yellow, or red. That is a sure route to dependency. We are our own motivators, and if we do not use our strength, our intelligence, and our determination to achieve what we are capable of doing, the fault lies with us, not with some anonymous "white male establishment."

Of course, laws were created to prevent such self-directed lives on the part of women—men are all too often terrified of women and have historically tried to keep us in a non-threatening mode—but now that laws no longer coerce us in the workplace or compel us to stay at home, we have no excuse except personal laziness or lack of self confidence. If it requires superb quality to rise to the top, that is only a stimulant, not a limitation.

The subject of sexual harassment is also a cop-out. A good firm no, with the implication that it might be followed up by a knee to the groin, works wonders if the woman has not been brainwashed into believing she cannot or should not reply in that manner. So you need that job? No, you don't—you need *A* job, and that isn't the right one.

Women can hurt men, when whittle comes to cut. Not in a fist-fight, for our reach is often short, and few of us have the upper body strength for that kind of nonsense. But a kick to the knee or a thumb in the eye or a mist of hair spray in the face can work wonders, when needed. Instead of preaching victimology, the feminist movement should push for defensive training for girls (for all children, actually). That would remove most of the problems right there.

I have spoken with young women who all but walk in fetal position, fearing attack from some amorphous "they" at every step. When I give them some mean old lady advice, they look at me wide-eyed and say, "But that would HURT him!"

To which I reply, "What the hell do you think an attacker is going to do to you?"

There is no excuse for lack of effort, be it professionally, educationally, or physically, when the time comes. My grandmother used to say that a lady does the best she can with whatever she has, no matter what the circumstances.

So you are afraid of being unladylike? Nonsense! A lady will kick that sucker where it hurts, every time, instead of submitting to injustice or indignity. That is the way to remain a lady, instead of becoming a victim.

XXI.

MOST RECENT YEARS

I had been writing with frantic speed for many years, driven not only by my compulsion to tell stories but by need for money caused by Joe's seven-year illness. By 1999 I had begun to flag, and when Joe died late that year I felt like a deflated balloon. Even if I had not had a wreck the next month, I am sure that my internal writing pressure would still have dwindled to a slight hiss.

Since then I have written very little. For a long time, just the thought of starting a new book made me want to scream and run. I have written several very strange short stories in the years between then and now, but even those come at long intervals.

That doesn't mean that strange things don't keep happening to me, however. Living this far out in the country, I have all sorts of critters sharing my property and sometimes my deck. Pickups fly low down the hard-top road in front of my house, boat trailers bouncing behind them. In summer choppers sometimes quarter the area on both sides of the river, probably searching for plantings of marijuana.

Nobody bothers this old lady, however. It is well known that I have guns in my house within arm's reach, and would not hesitate to use them on anyone appearing in the middle of the night or with the wrong attitude.

XXII.

A FINAL NOTE AS OF 2008

I never expected to live this long, or even wanted to. Yet I am still living alone, healthy and fairly active. This year, the Science Fiction Writers of America chose me as their Author Emeritus, which surprised the heck out of me. In the past few months I have sold several recently written short stories to anthologies as well. Evidently fate still has a use for me, though at this point I feel like a pretty bad waste of skin. We will see what happens next! And when I die, I expect to fly free through the universe, learning answers to all my questions.

A. M.

A BIBLIOGRAPHY OF THE BOOKS OF ARDATH MAYHAR

COMPILED BY ROBERT REGINALD

(All bylines are as by "Ardath Mayhar," unless otherwise noted; series names are listed in small capital letters)

Journey to an Ending, by "Ardath Frances Hurst." Fort Smith, AR: South and West, 1965. [poetry collection]
How the Gods Wove in Kyrannon. Garden City, NY: Doubleday & Co., Oct. 1979. TALES OF THE TRIPLE MOONS. [fantasy novel]
The Seekers of Shar-Nuhn. Garden City, NY: Doubleday & Co., July 1980. TALES OF THE TRIPLE MOONS. [fantasy novel]
Soul-Singer of Tyrnos. New York: Atheneum, Aug. 1981. [fantasy novel]
Warlock's Gift. Garden City, NY: Doubleday & Co., Apr. 1982. TALES OF THE TRIPLE MOONS. [fantasy novel]
Runes of the Lyre. New York: Atheneum, Sept. 1982. [fantasy novel]
Golden Dream: A Fuzzy Odyssey. New York: Ace Books, Oct. 1982. FUZZIES SERIES. [science fiction novel]

Lords of the Triple Moons. New York: Atheneum, Feb. 1983. TALES OF THE TRIPLE MOONS. [fantasy novel]

Khi to Freedom. New York: Ace Books, May 1983. [science fiction novel]

The Absolutely Perfect Horse, with Marylois Dunn. New York: Harper & Row, June 1983. [young adult novel with East Texas setting]

Exile on Vlahil. Garden City, NY: Doubleday & Co., May 1984. [science fiction novel]

The World Ends in Hickory Hollow. Garden City, NY: Doubleday & Co., Mar. 1985. [near future novel with East Texas setting]

The Saga of Grittel Sundotha. New York: Atheneum, Apr. 1985. [fantasy novel]

Medicine Walk. New York: Atheneum, Sept. 1985. BURR HENDERSON #1. [young adult novel]

Carrots and Miggle. New York: Atheneum, Mar. 1986. [young adult novel with East Texas setting]

Makra Choria. New York: Atheneum, Mar. 1987. [fantasy novel]

The Sword and the Dagger. Chicago, IL: FASA Corp., May 1987. BATTLETECH SERIES. [science fiction novel]

Trail of the Seahawks, with Ron Fortier. Lake Geneva, WI: TSR, June 1987. MACAQUE CYCLE #2. [science fiction novel]

The Wall. New York: Space and Time, July 1987. [horror novel]

Feud at Sweetwater Creek, as "Frank Cannon." New York: Zebra Books, Aug. 1987. as: *Feud at Sweetwater Creek: A Novel of the Old West*, by "Ardath Mayhar." Rockville, MD: The Borgo Press, June 2007. [western novel]

Bloody Texas Trail, as "Frank Cannon." New York: Zebra Books, Mar. 1988. as: *The Heirs of Three Oaks: A Novel of the Old West*, by "Ardath Mayhar." Rockville, MD: The Borgo Press, Oct. 2007. [western novel]

A Place of Silver Silence. New York: Walker & Co., Oct. 1988. [young adult science fiction novel]

Texas Gunsmoke, as "Frank Cannon." New York: Zebra Books, Oct. 1988. as: *Prescription for Danger: A Novel of the Old West*, by "Ardath Mayhar." Rockville, MD: The Borgo Press, Apr. 2007. [western novel]

Monkey Station, with Ron Fortier. Lake Geneva, WI: TSR, July 1989. MACAQUE CYCLE #1. [science fiction novel]

People of the Mesa. New York: Diamond/Charter, Mar. 1992. [AmerIndian historical novel]

Wild Country, as "John Killdeer." New York: Bantam Books, Mar. 1992. MOUNTAIN MAJESTY #1. [western novel]

The Untamed, as "John Killdeer." New York: Bantam Books, June 1992. MOUNTAIN MAJESTY #2. [western novel]

Wilderness Rendezvous, as "John Killdeer." New York: Bantam Books, Nov. 1992. MOUNTAIN MAJESTY #3. [western novel]

Blood Kin, as "John Killdeer." New York: Bantam Books, Feb. 1993. MOUNTAIN MAJESTY #4. [western novel]

Island in the Lake. New York: Diamond/Charter, June 1993. [AmerIndian historical novel]

Passage West, by "John Killdeer." New York: Bantam Books, Jan. 1994. MOUNTAIN MAJESTY #5. [western novel]

Towers of the Earth. New York: Diamond Books, Feb. 1994. [AmerIndian historical novel]

The Far Horizon, as "John Killdeer." New York: Bantam Books, July 1994. MOUNTAIN MAJESTY #6. [western novel]

Mean Little Old Lady at Work: The Selected Works of Ardath Mayhar. Concord, CA: Dark Regions Press, 1994. [short story collection]

Hunters of the Plains. New York: Berkley Books, Apr. 1995. [AmerIndian historical novel]

Slewfoot Sally and the Flying Mule and Other Tales from Cotton County. Kingwood, TX: Blue Lantern Publishing, May 1995. as: *Slewfoot Sally and the Flying Mule: Tall Tales from Cotton County, Texas*. Rockville, MD: The Borgo Press, Jan. 2009. [fantasy collection]

Reflections: Published and Unpublished Poetry. [Chireno, TX: Ardath Mayhar], 1995. [poetry collection]

High Mountain Winter, as "Frances Hurst." New York: Berkley Books, Mar. 1996. as: *High Mountain Winter: A Novel of the Old West*, by "Ardath Mayhar." Rockville, MD: The Borgo Press, Fall 2009. [western novel]

Through a Stone Wall: A Book on Writing. Kingwood, TX: Blue Lantern Publishing, 1996. [nonfiction]

Timber Pirates, with Marylois Dunn. Kingwood, TX: Blue Lantern Publishing, Jan. 1997. [young adult novel with East Texas setting]

A Road of Stars: A Tale of Art and Death. Princeton, NJ: Xlibris Corp., Aug. 1998. [fantasy novel]

Polarities, with Jerri S. Richards. Kingwood, TX: Blue Lantern Publishing, Jan. 2000. [poetry collection]

The Snowlost/Exile on Vlahil: Being a Tale of Man and Moohl, Who Found Themselves Compatible. St. Paul, MN: Stone Dragon Press, Dec. 2000. Two novels, one

(*The Snowlost*) published for the first time. [science fiction novel collection]

Riddles & Dreams: The Exiles of Damaria, Book I. Staten Island, NY: Images Publishing, June 2003. THE EXILES OF DAMARIA #1. [fantasy novel]

Witchfire, with Ron Fortier. Lafayette, LA: Cornerstone Book Publishers, Sept. 2007. [horror novel]

Reflections; &, Journey to an Ending: Collected Poems. Rockville, MD: The Borgo Press, Dec. 2008. Includes the contents of the previously-published books, *Reflections* and *Journey to an Ending*. [poetry collection]

Through a Stone Wall: Lessons from Thirty Years of Writing, Second Edition. Rockville, MD: The Borgo Press, Jan. 2009. A revised and expanded edition of *Through a Stone Wall*. [nonfiction]

Medicine Dream: Being the Further Adventures of Burr Henderson: A Sequel to Medicine Walk. Rockville, MD: The Borgo Press, Jan. 2009. BURR HENDERSON #2. [young adult novel]

The Tulpa: A Novel of Fantasy. Rockville, MD: The Borgo Press, Jan. 2009. [young adult fantasy novel]

A Planet Called Heaven: A Science Fiction Novel. Rockville, MD: The Borgo Press, Feb. 2009. [science fiction novel]

The Door in the Hill: A Tale of the Turnipins. Rockville, MD: The Borgo Press, Feb. 2009. [young adult fantasy novel]

Messengers in White: A Science Fantasy Novel. Rockville, MD: The Borgo Press, Feb. 2009. [fantasy novel]

The Dropouts: A Tale of Growing Up in East Texas. Rockville, MD: The Borgo Press, Mar. 2009. [young adult novel with East Texas setting]

Lone Runner: A Novel of the Old West. Rockville, MD: The Borgo Press, Mar. 2009. This is the author's last completed novel to date. [western novel]

Deadly Memoir: A Novel of Suspense. Rockville, MD: The Borgo Press, Mar. 2009. [suspense novel]

The Fugitives: A Tale of Prehistoric Times. Rockville, MD: The Borgo Press, Mar. 2009. [young adult Amer-Indian historical novel]

The Lintons of Skillet Bend: A Novel of East Texas. Rockville, MD: The Borgo Press, Mar. 2009. [young adult novel with East Texas setting]

Two-Moons and the Black Tower: A Novel of Fantasy. Rockville, MD: The Borgo Press, Mar. 2009. [fantasy novel]

Crazy Quilt: The Best Short Stories of Ardath Mayhar. Rockville, MD: The Borgo Press, Apr. 2009. [fantasy and horror story collection]

Strange Doin's in the Pine Hills: Stories of Fantasy and Mystery in East Texas. Rockville, MD: The Borgo Press, June 2009. [fantasy and mystery story collection]

Closely Knit in Scarlatt: A Novel of Suspense. Rockville, MD: The Borgo Press, July 2009. [suspense novel]

Death in the Square: A Washington Shipp Mystery. Rockville, MD: The Borgo Press, July 2009. WASH SHIPP #1. [mystery novel]

A World of Weirdities: Tales to Shiver By. Rockville, MD: The Borgo Press, July 2009. [fantasy and horror story collection]

The Body in the Swamp: A Washington Shipp Mystery. Rockville, MD: The Borgo Press, July 2009. WASH SHIPP #2. [mystery novel]

The Clarrington Heritage: A Gothic Tale of Terror. Rockville, MD: The Borgo Press, Aug. 2009. [gothic suspense novel]

Strange View from a Skewed Orbit: An Oddball Memoir. Rockville, MD: The Borgo Press, Aug. 2009. [autobiography]

Shock Treatment: An Account of Granary's War: A Science Fiction Novel. Rockville, MD: The Borgo Press, Fall 2009. [science fiction novel]

Vendetta: A Novel of the Old West. Rockville, MD: The Borgo Press, Fall 2009. [western novel]

Ships & Seekers: The Exiles of Damaria, Book II. Rockville, MD: The Borgo Press, Fall 2009. THE EXILES OF DAMARIA #2. [fantasy novel]

ABOUT THE AUTHOR

The author of seventy books, more than forty of them published commercially, **ARDATH MAYHAR** began her career in the early eighties with science fiction novels from Doubleday and TSR. Atheneum published several of her young adult and children's novels. Changing focus, she wrote westerns (as **Frank Cannon**) and mountain man novels (as **John Killdeer**), four prehistoric Indian books under her own name, and historical western *High Mountain Winter* under the byline **Frances Hurst**.

Recently she has been working with on-line publishers. *A Road of Stars* was her first original novel to appear in print-on-demand format. Many of her out-of-print titles are now available from e-publishers fictionwise.com and renebooks.com; many other novels are being published by the Borgo Press Imprint of Wildside Press and Amazon.com.

Now in her seventies, Mayhar was widowed in 1999, after forty-one years of marriage, and has four grown sons. She now works at home, writing short fiction and nonfiction, and doing book doctoring professionally. Her web pages can be found at:

w2.netdot.com/ardathm/

and

http://ofearna.us/books/mayhar.html

www.ingramcontent.com/pod-product-compliance
Lightning Source LLC
LaVergne TN
LVHW041624070426
835507LV00008B/433